Magic Jar

Adults Coloring Book

Thank you for purchasing our book! We hope you enjoy it and find it useful. If you have a moment, we would love it if you could leave a review so that other readers can hear your thoughts on the book. Thanks again and have a great day!

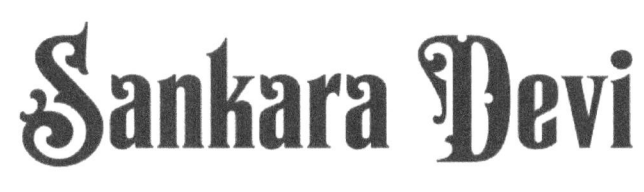

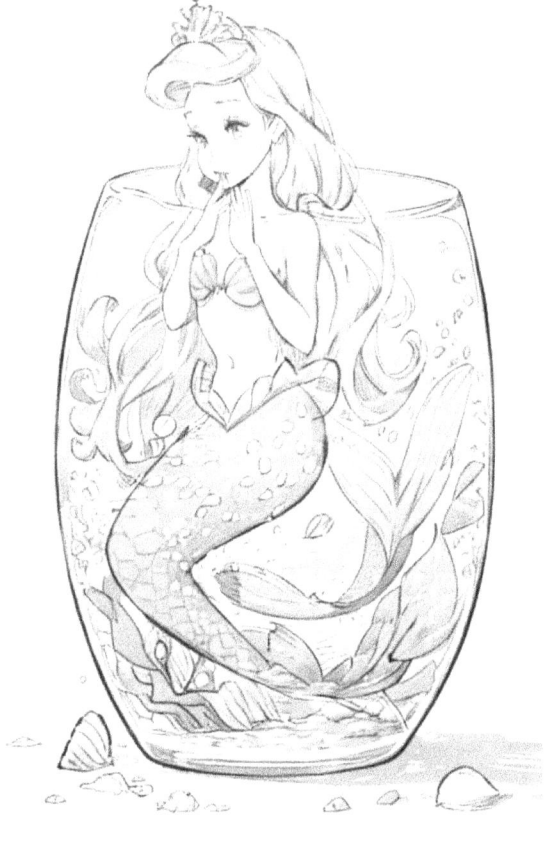

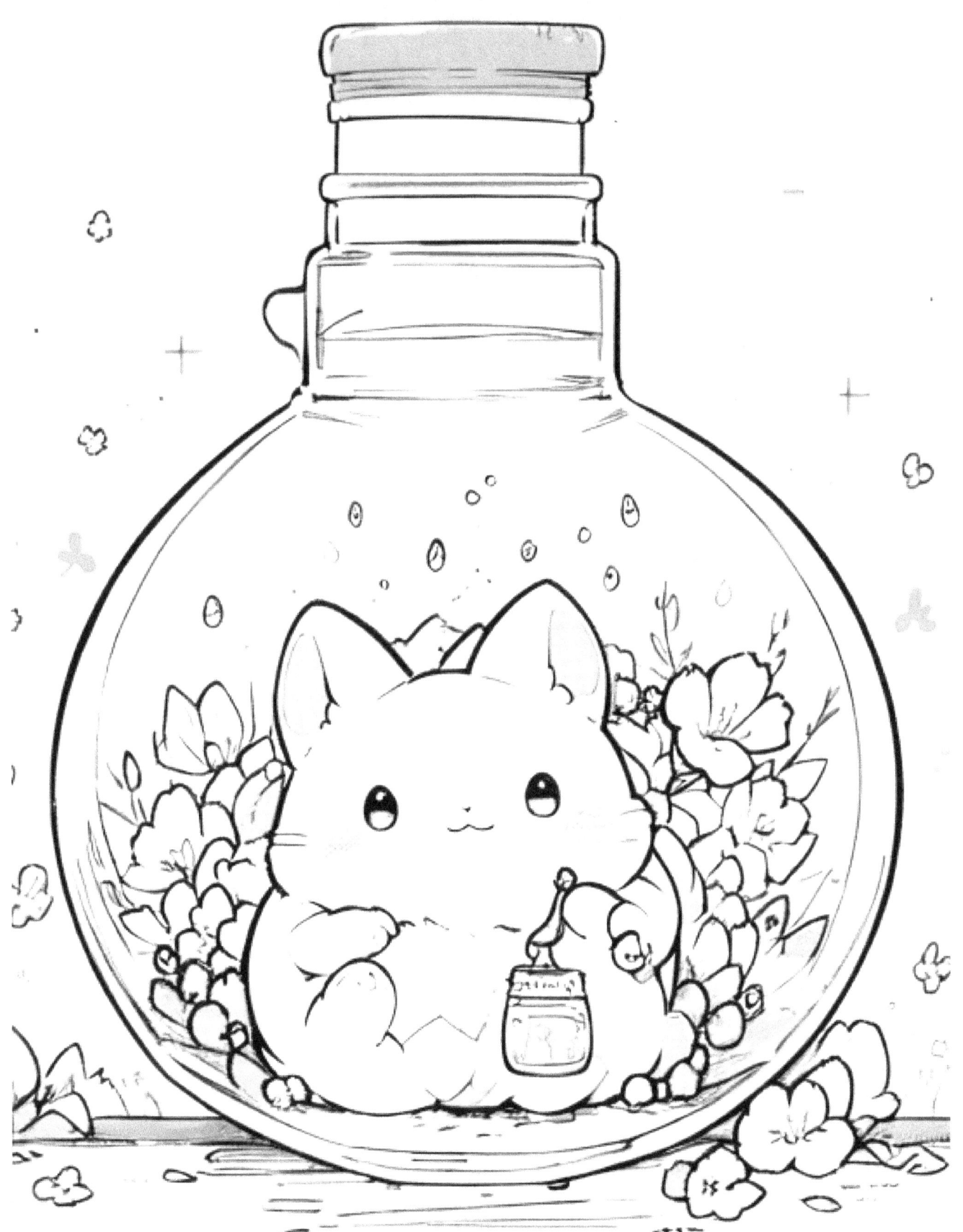

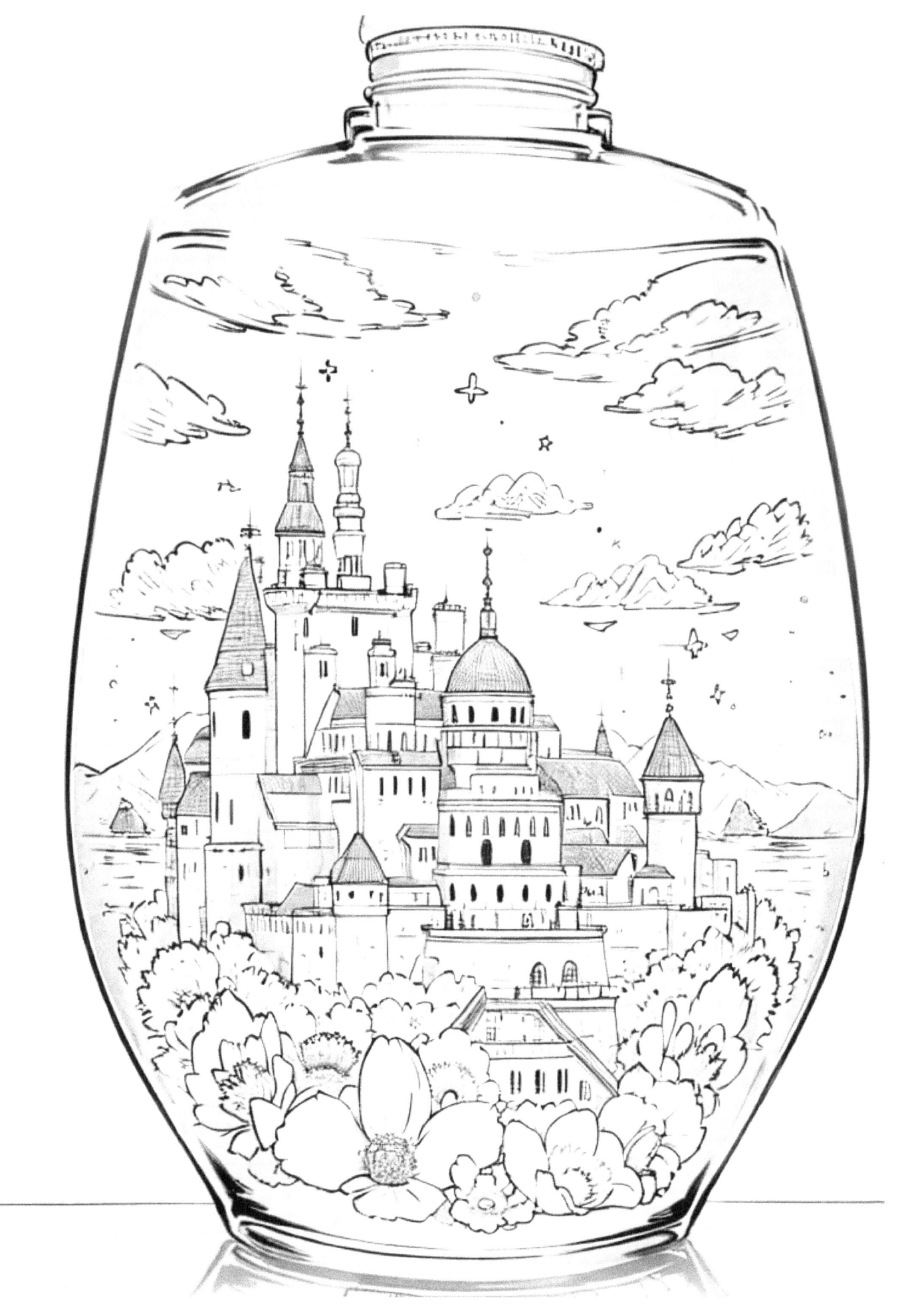

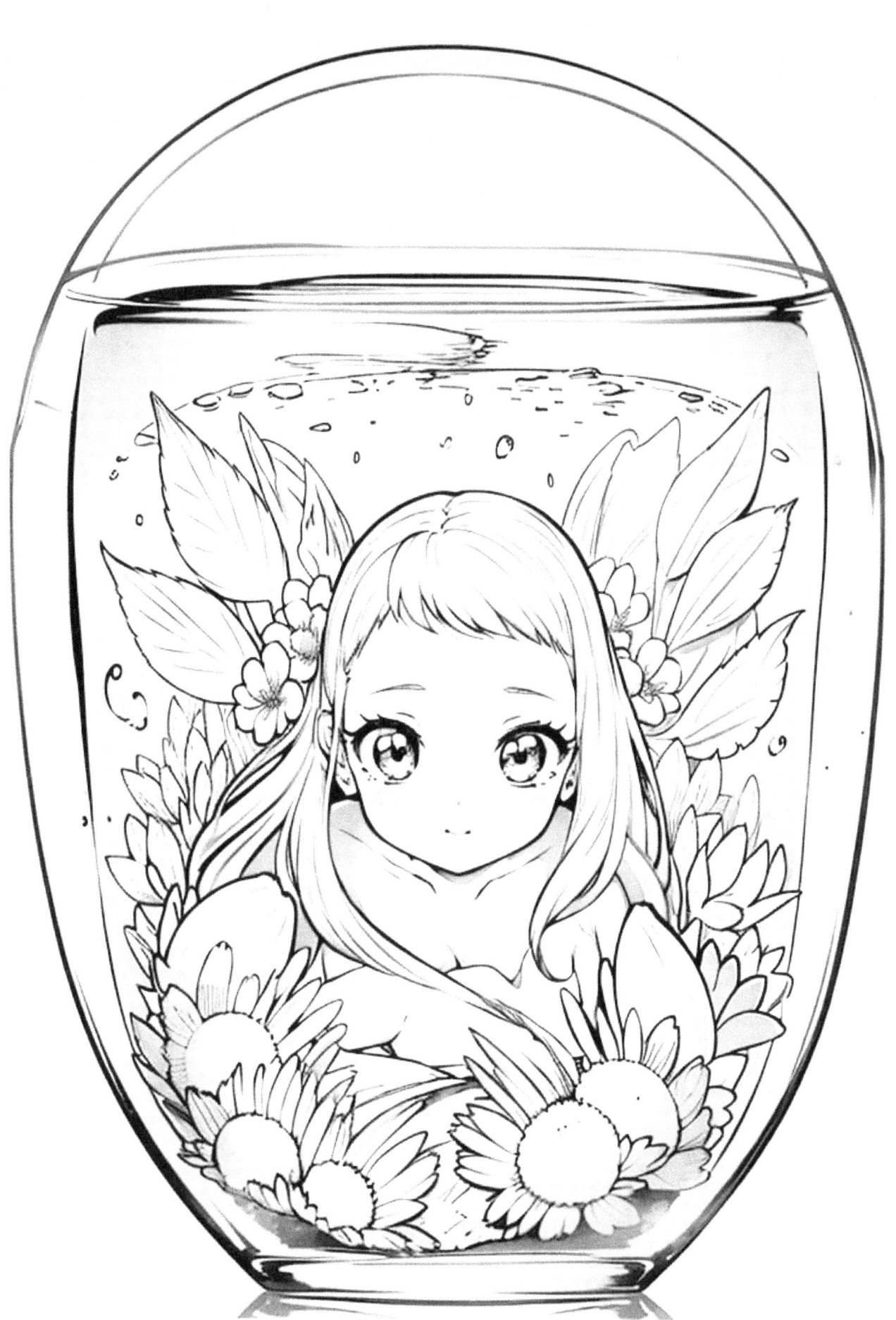

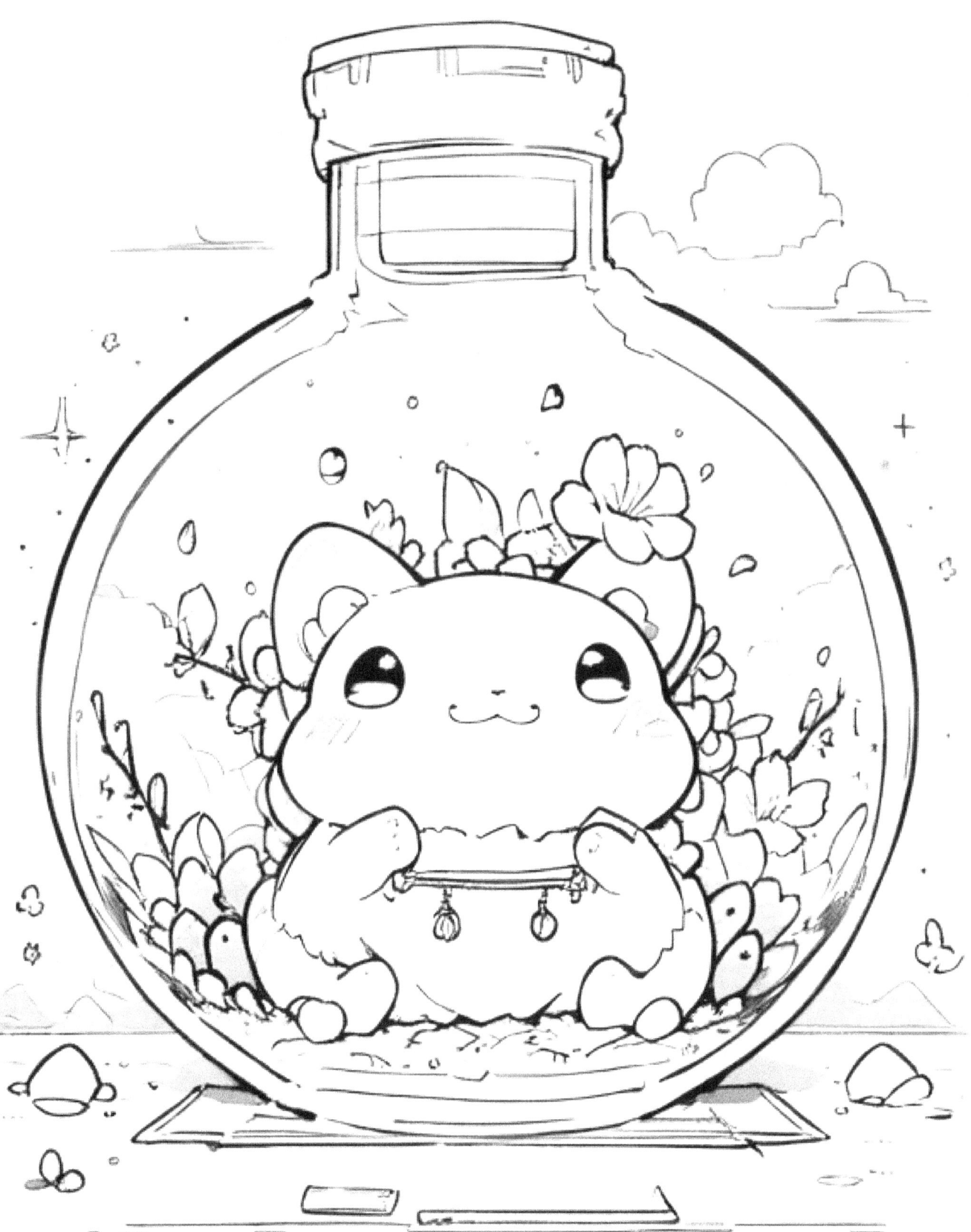

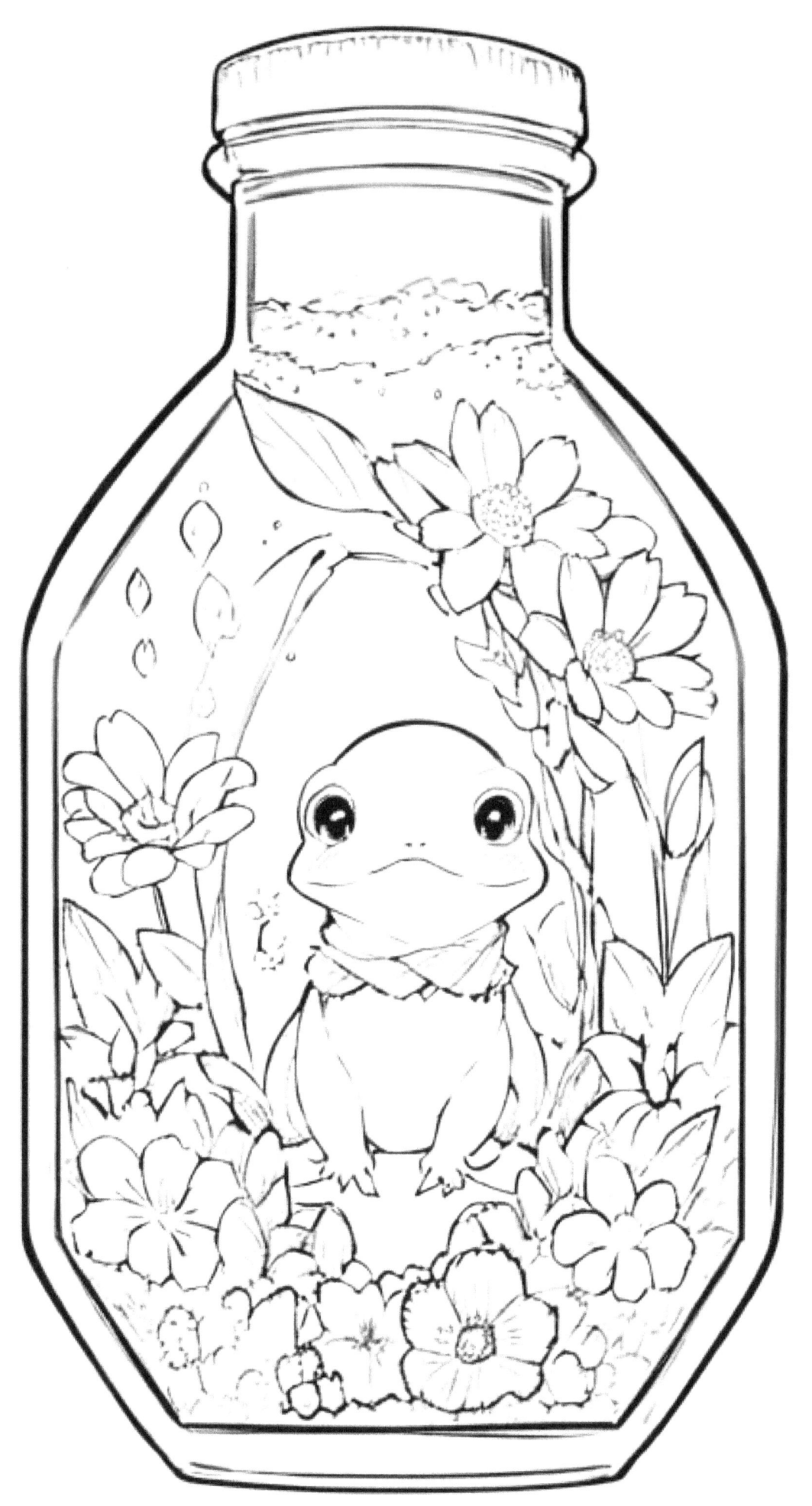

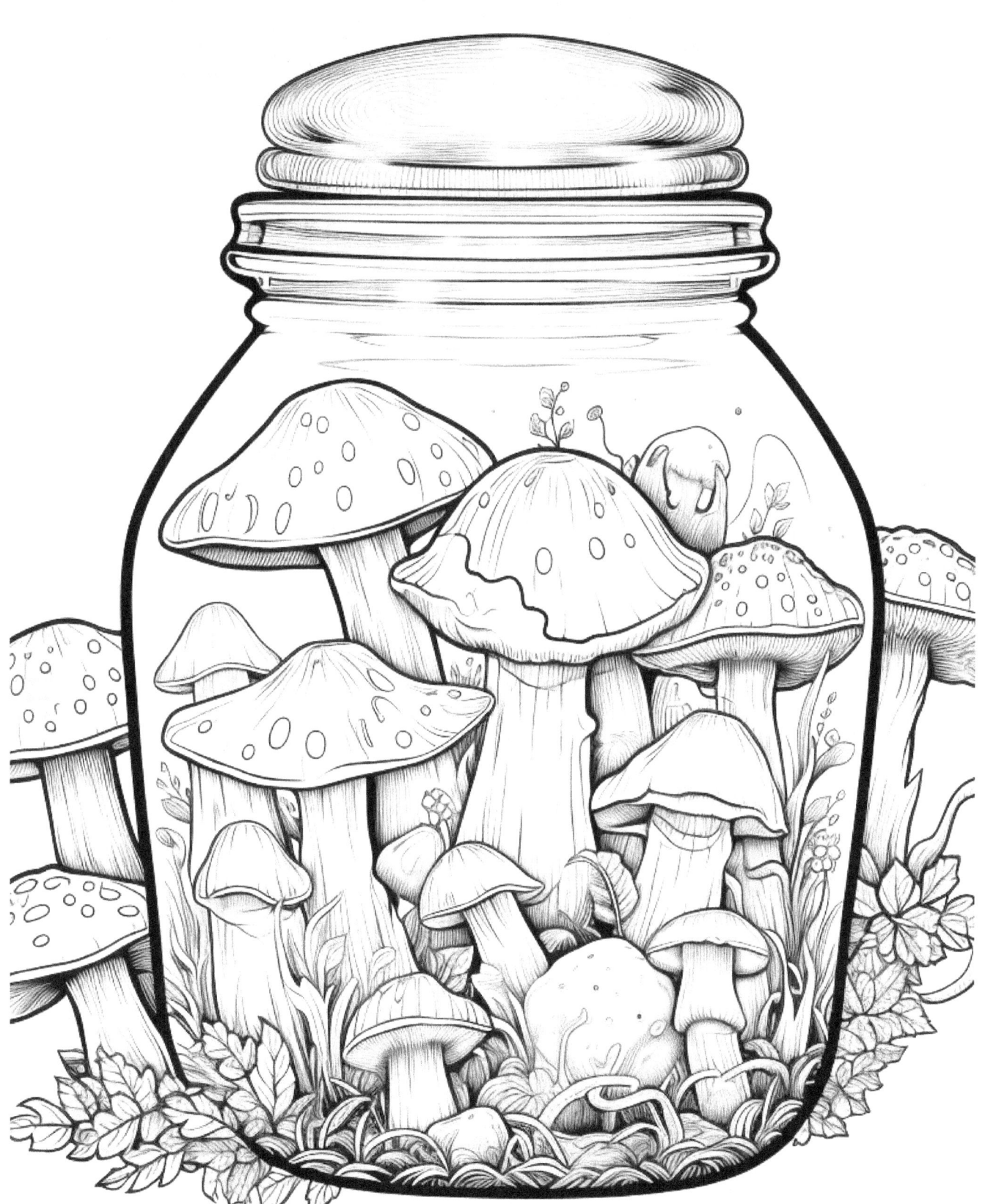

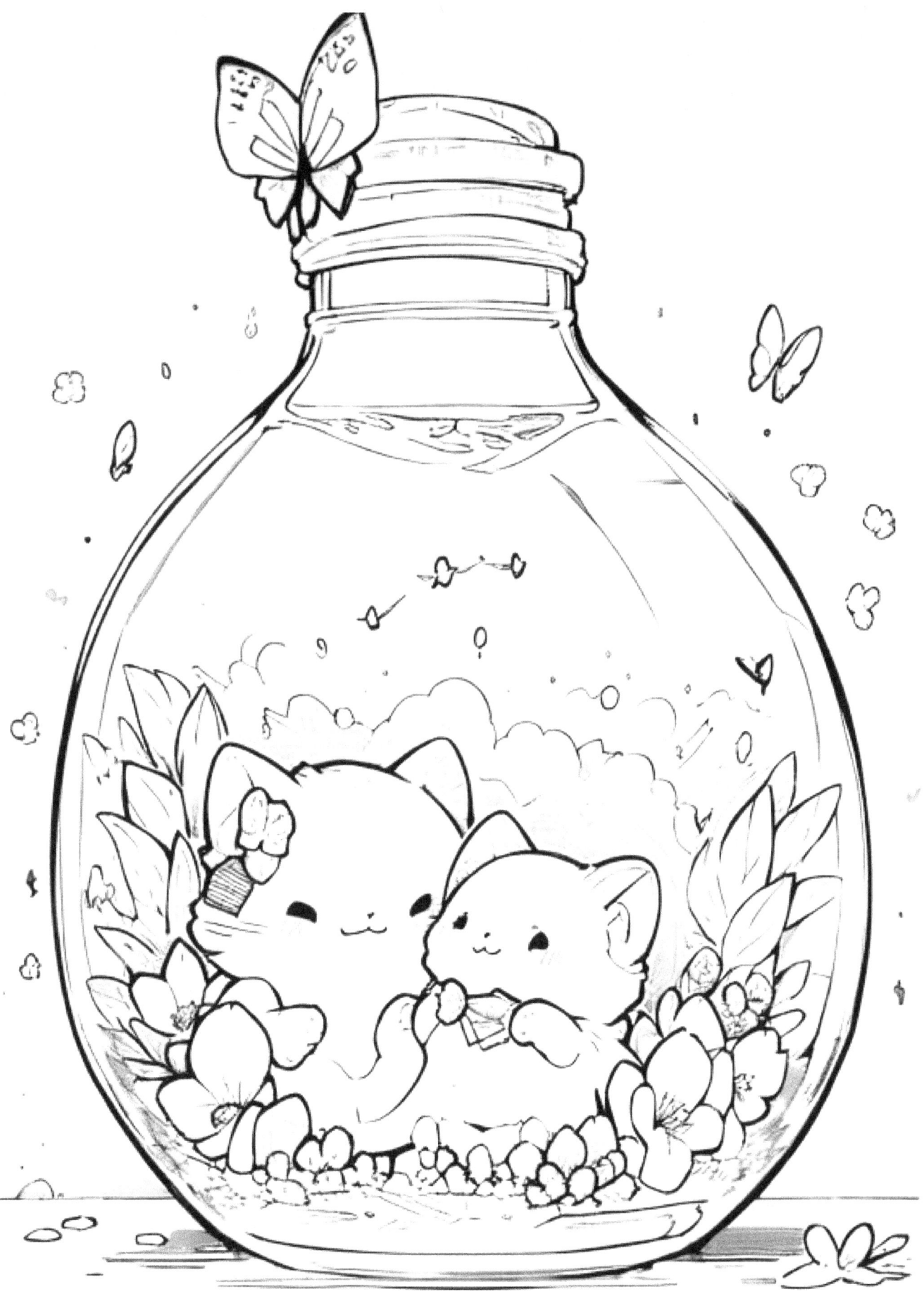

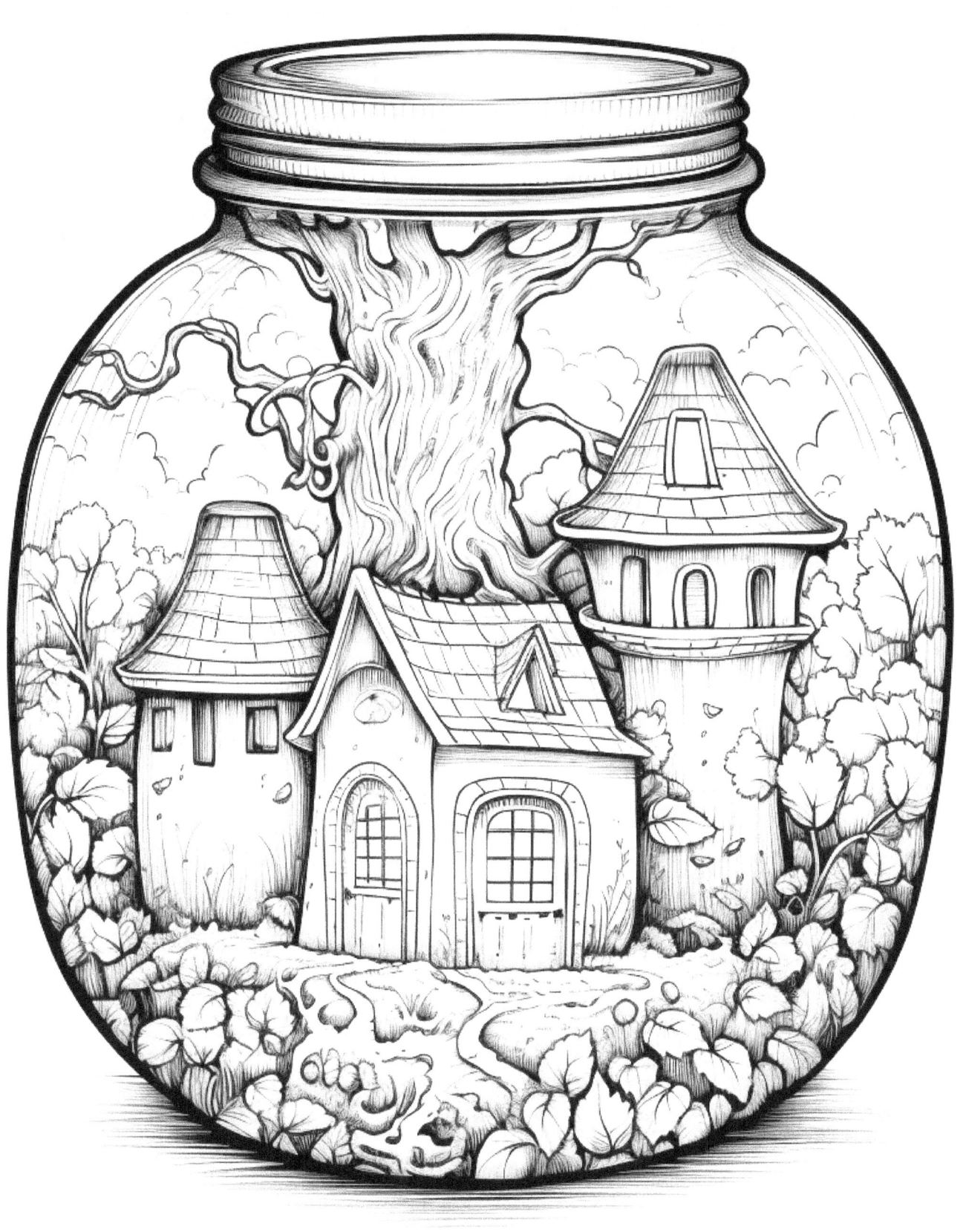

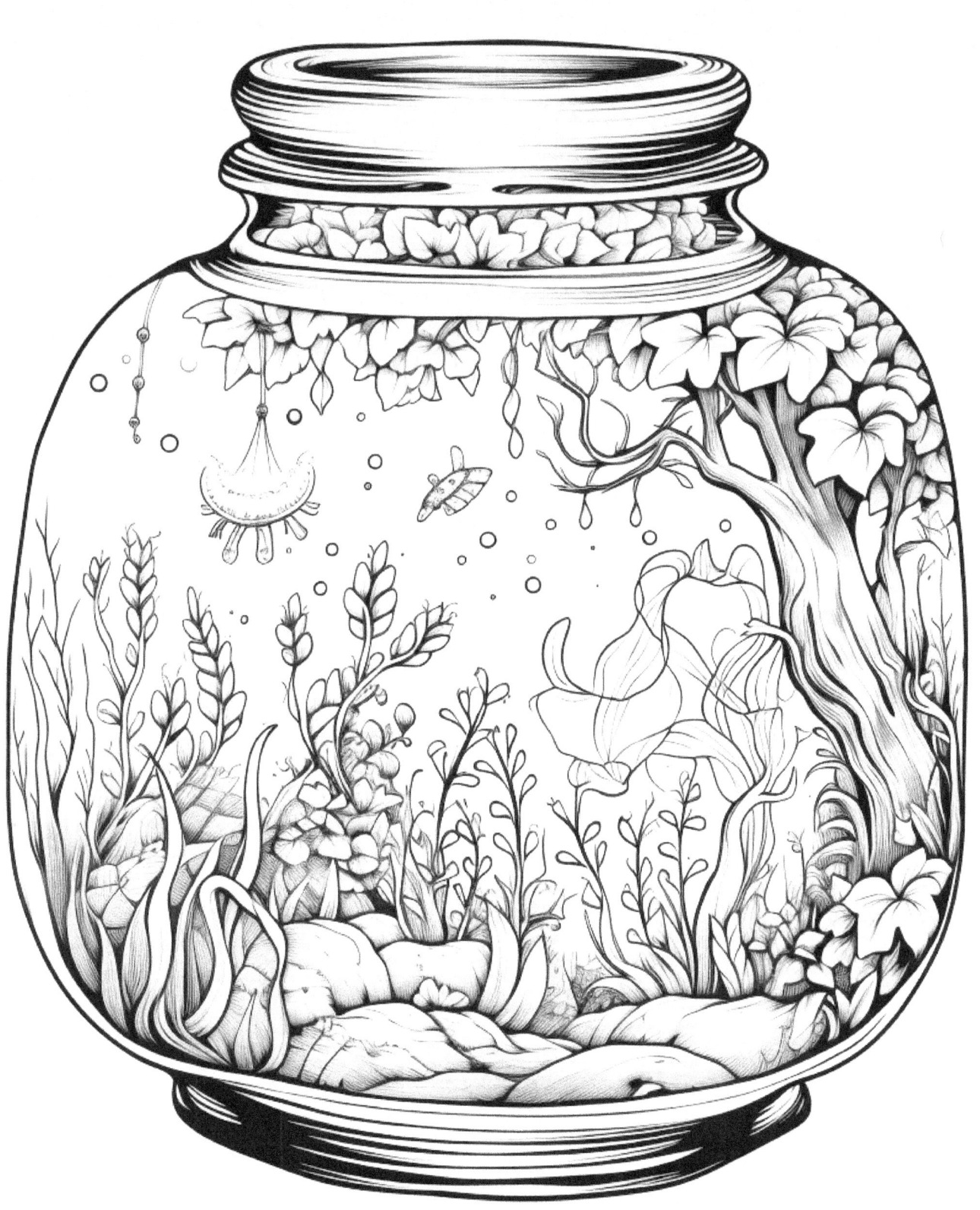

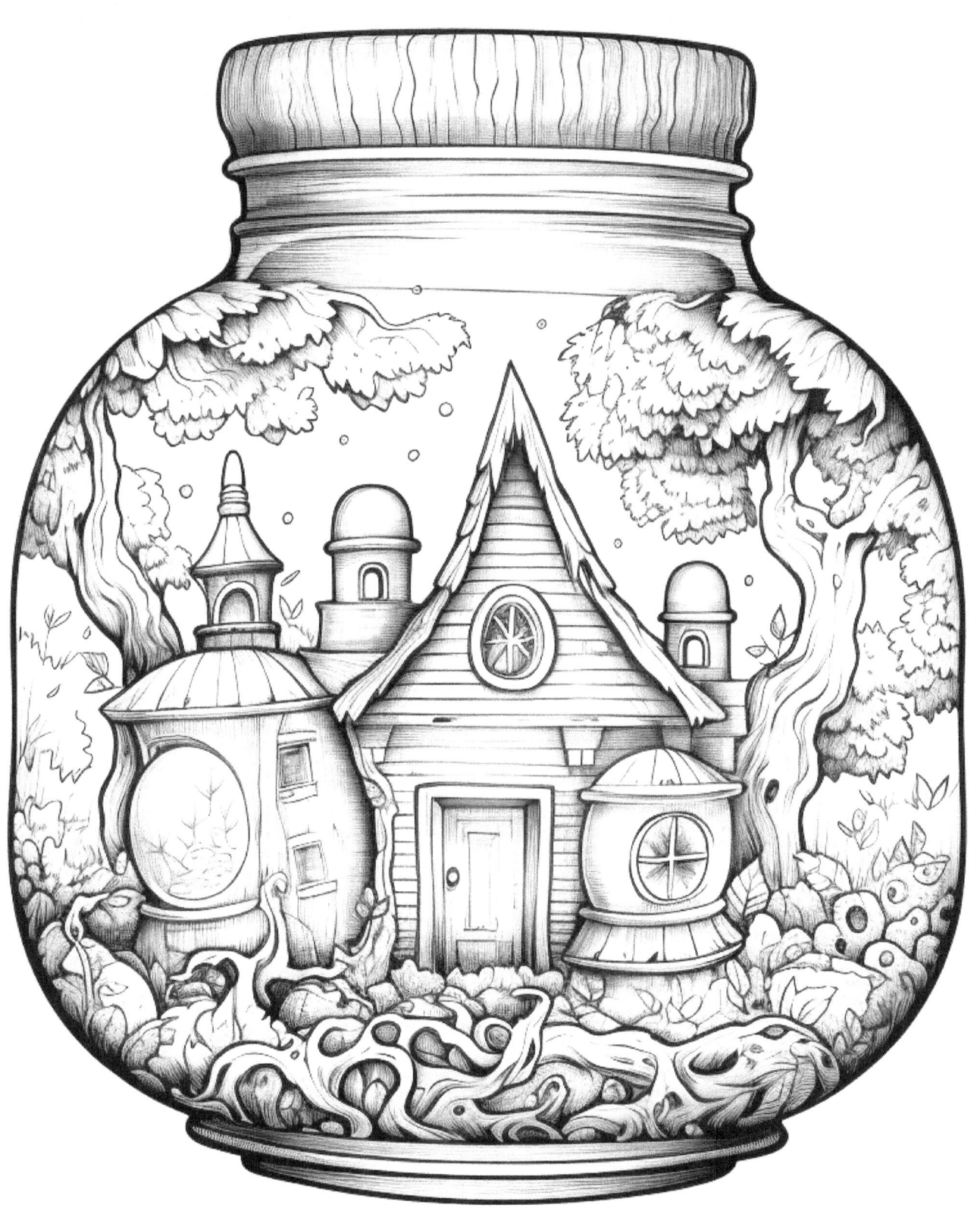

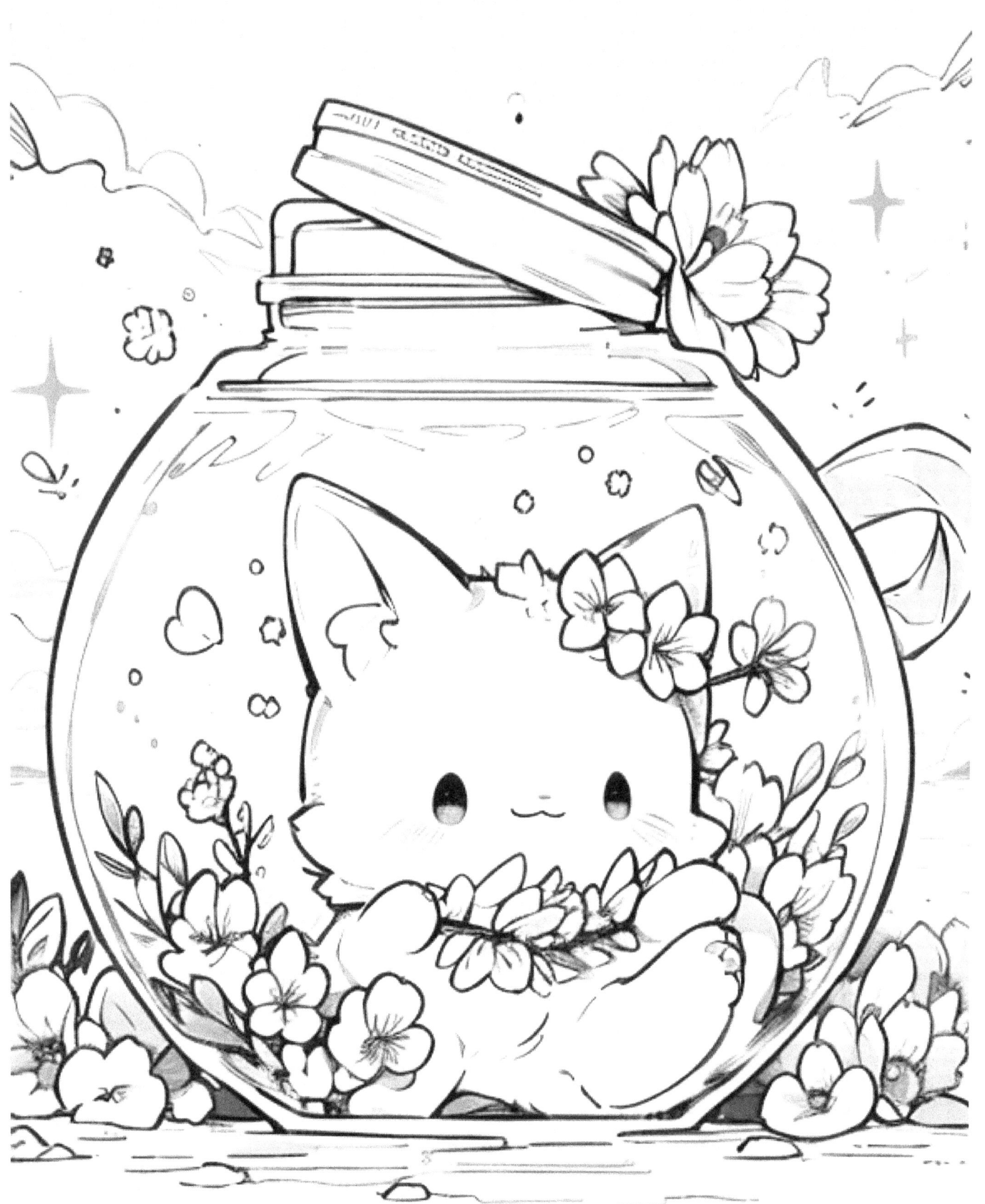

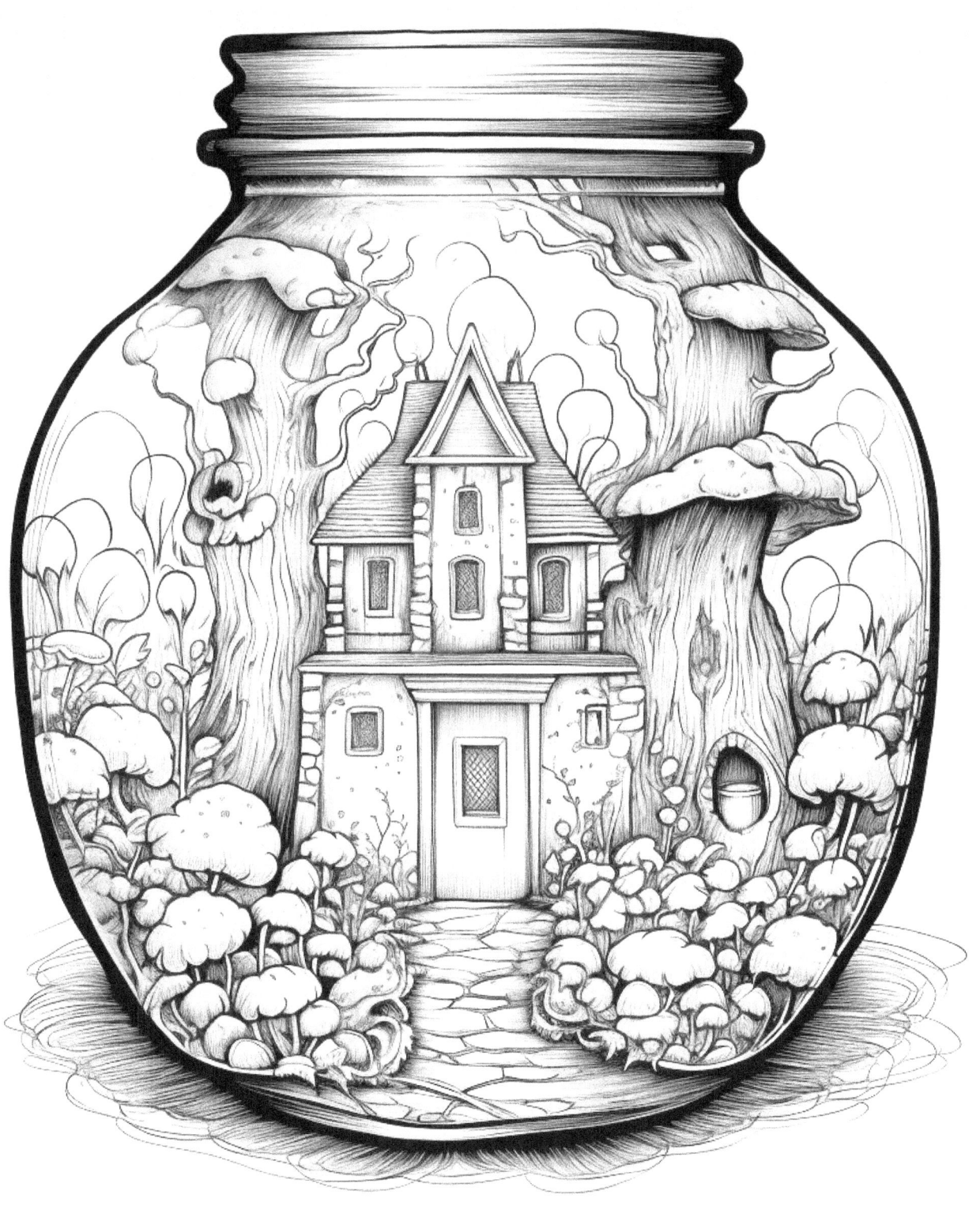

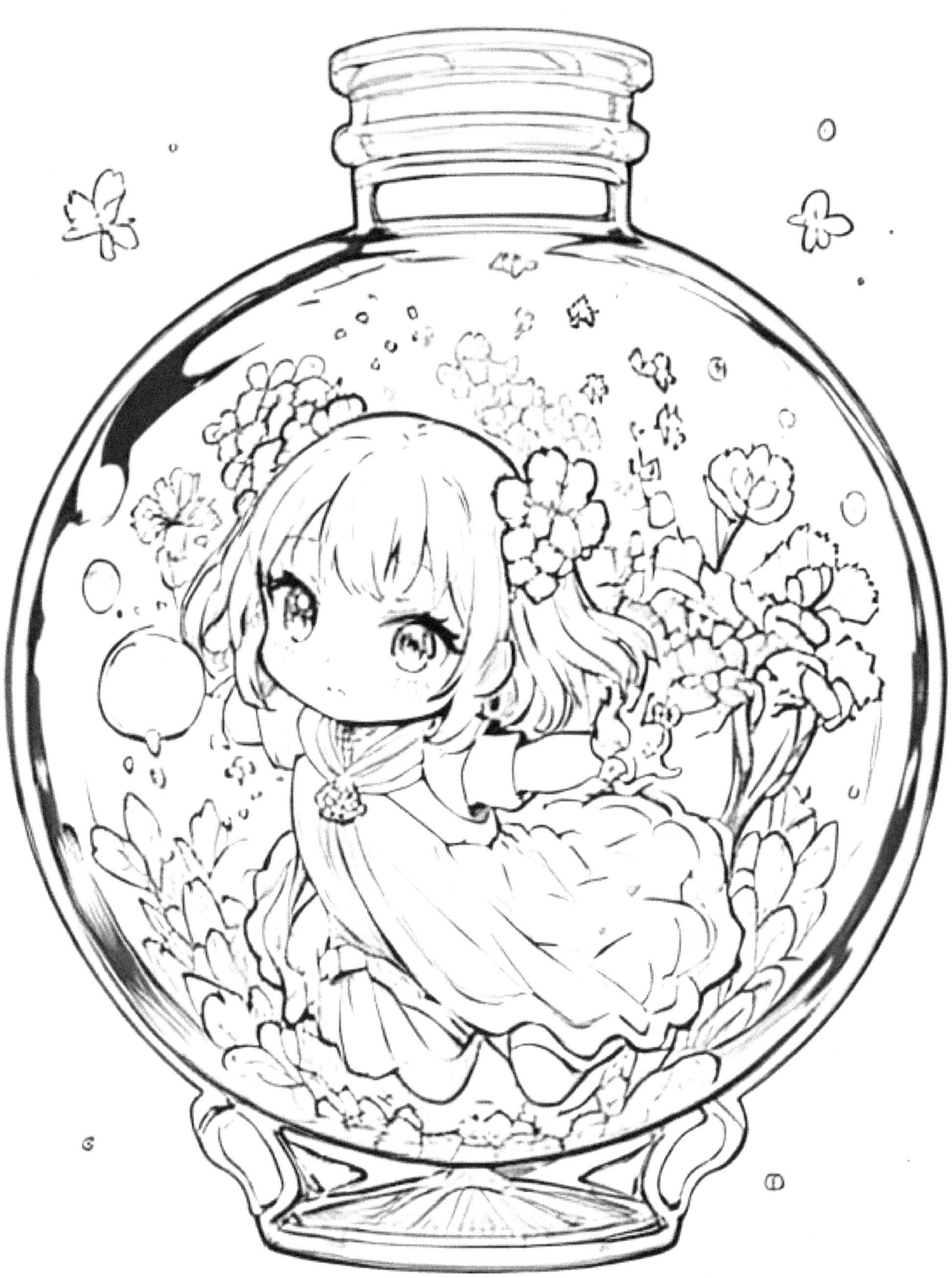

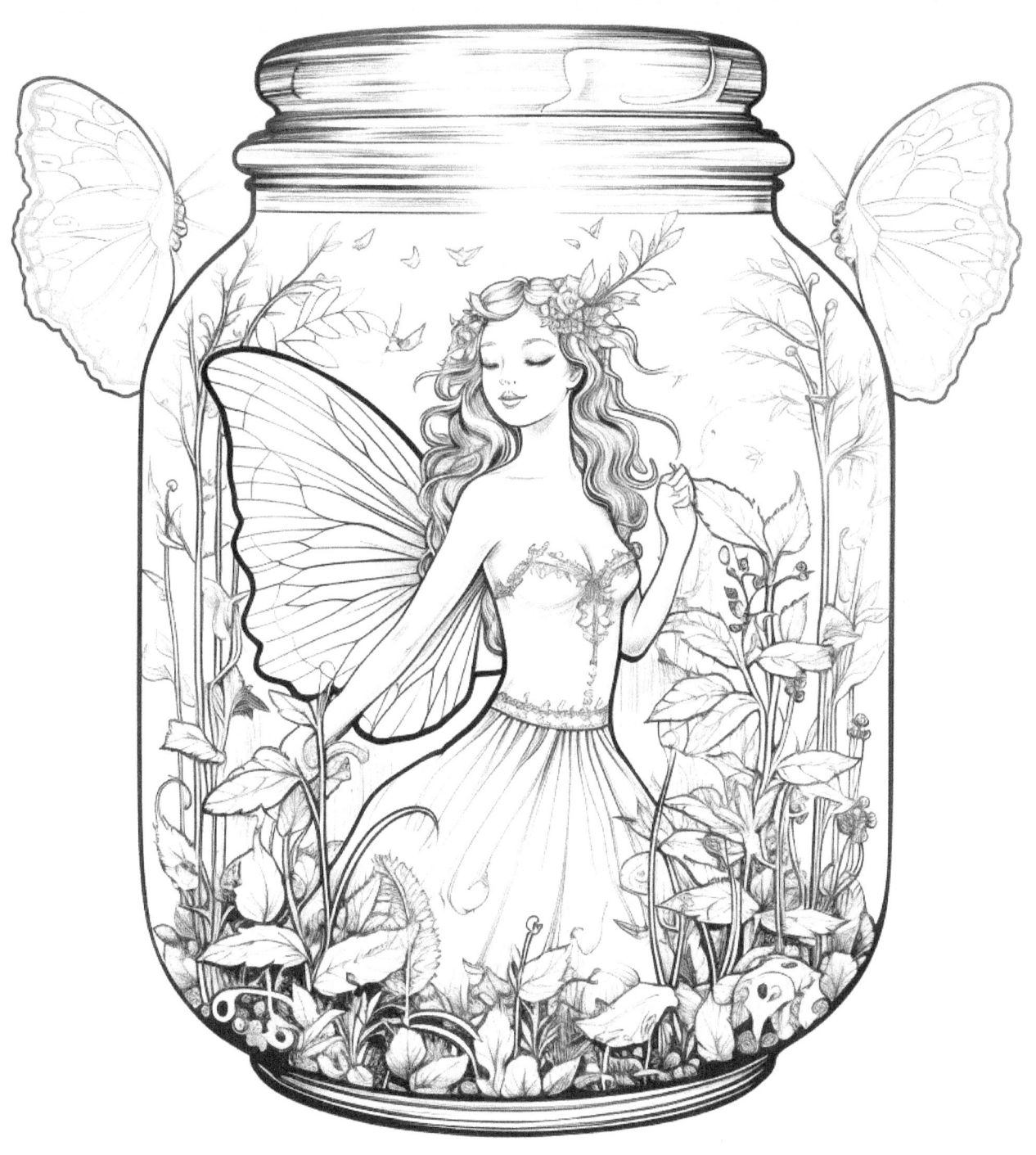

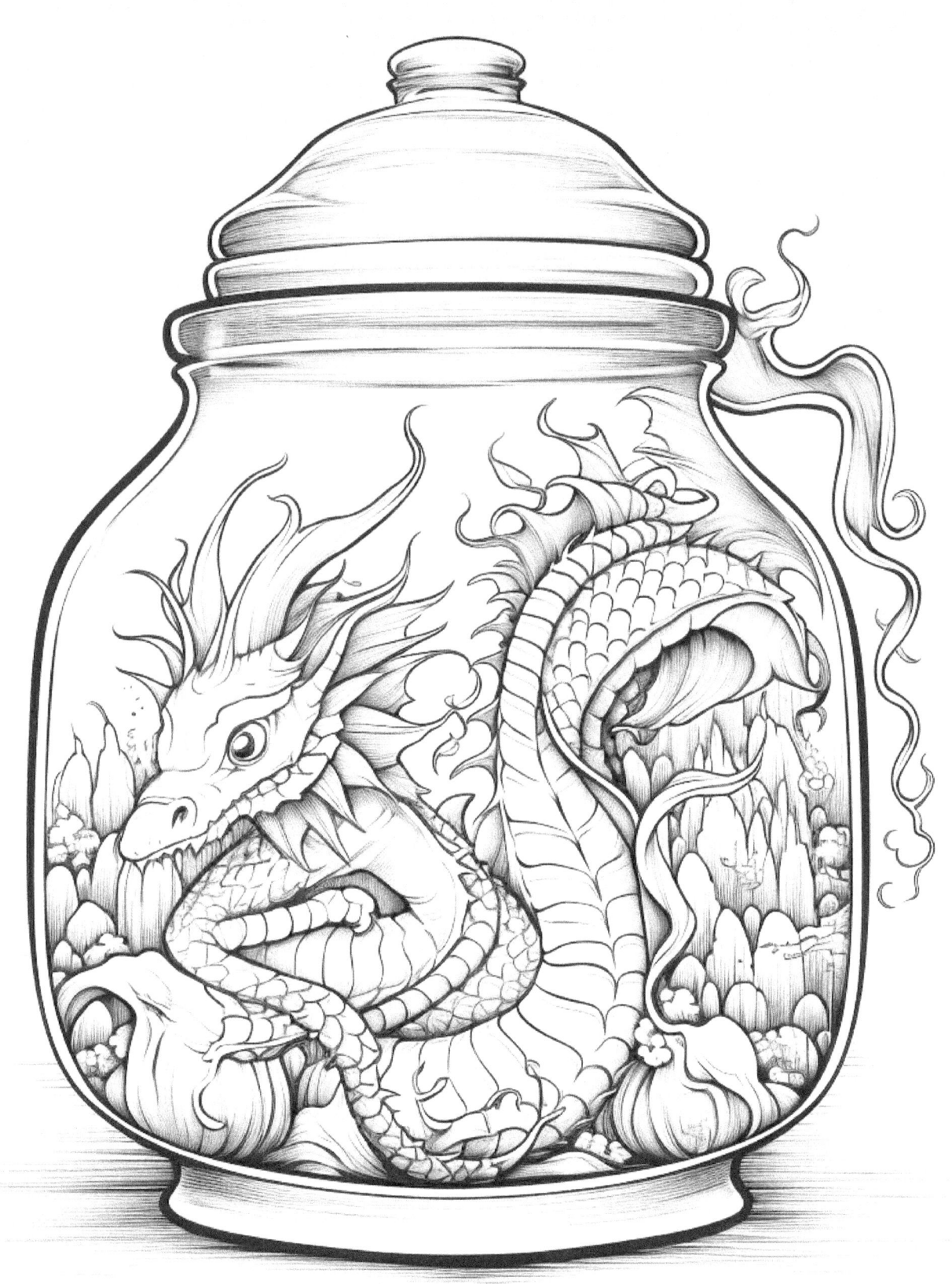

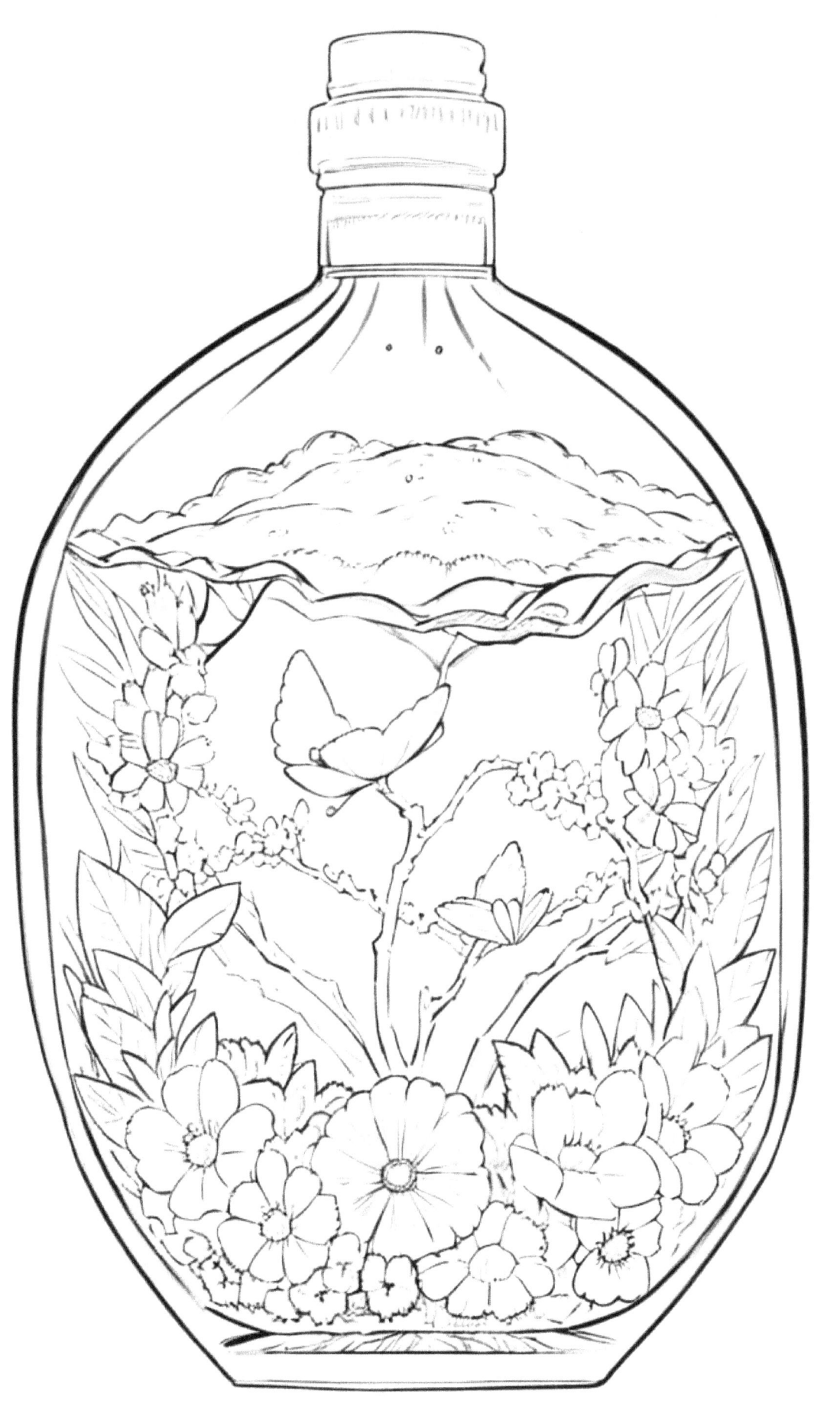

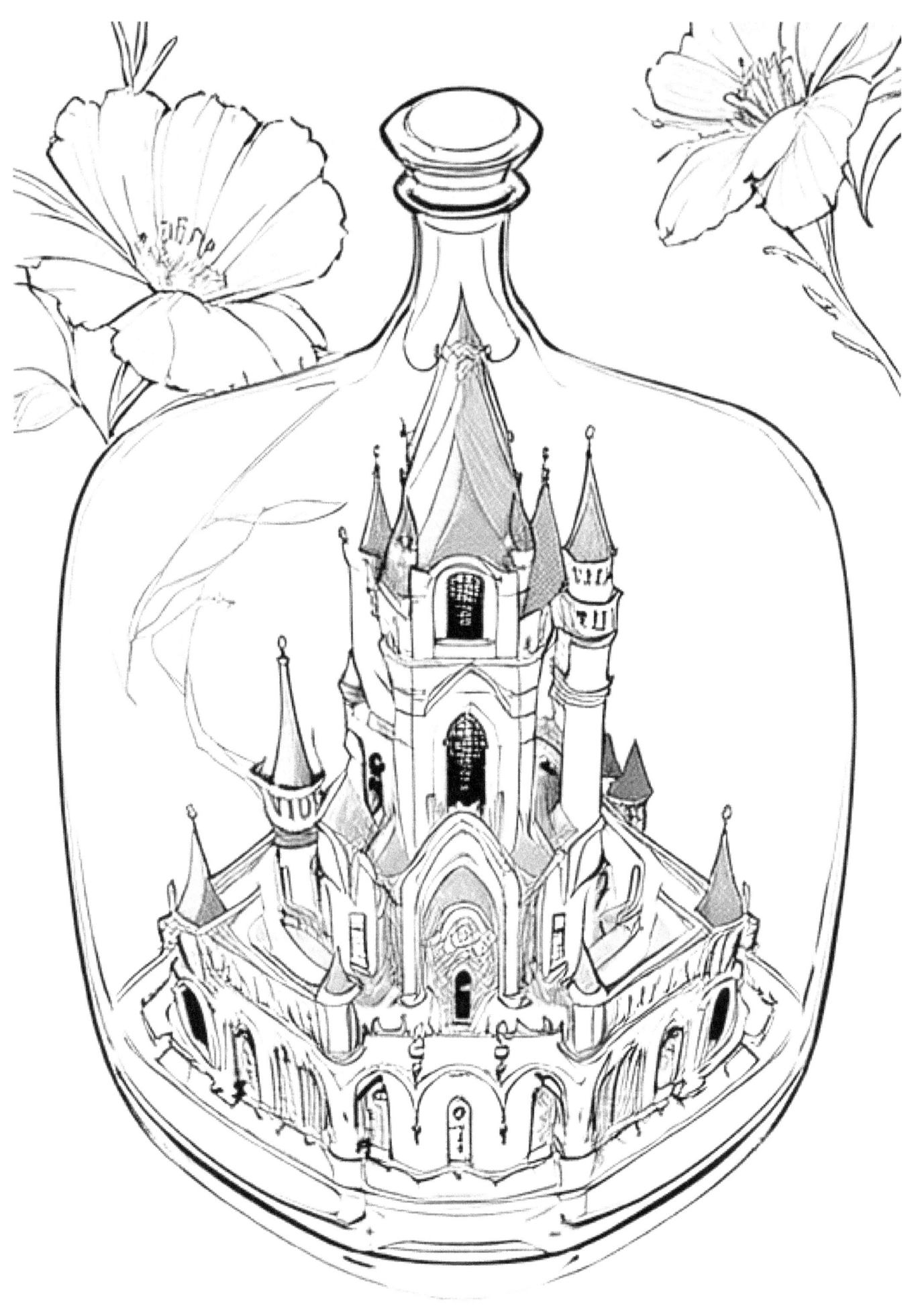

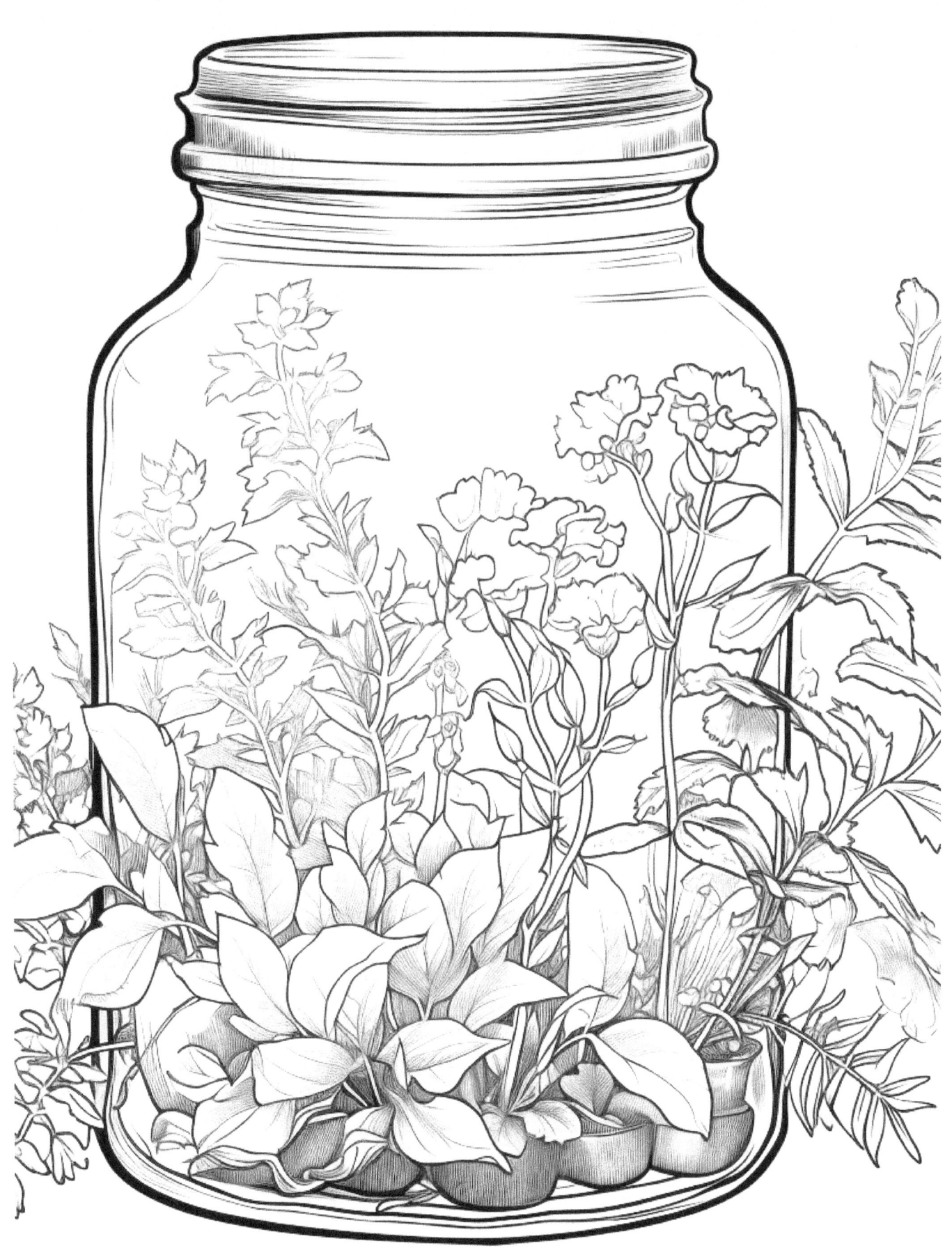

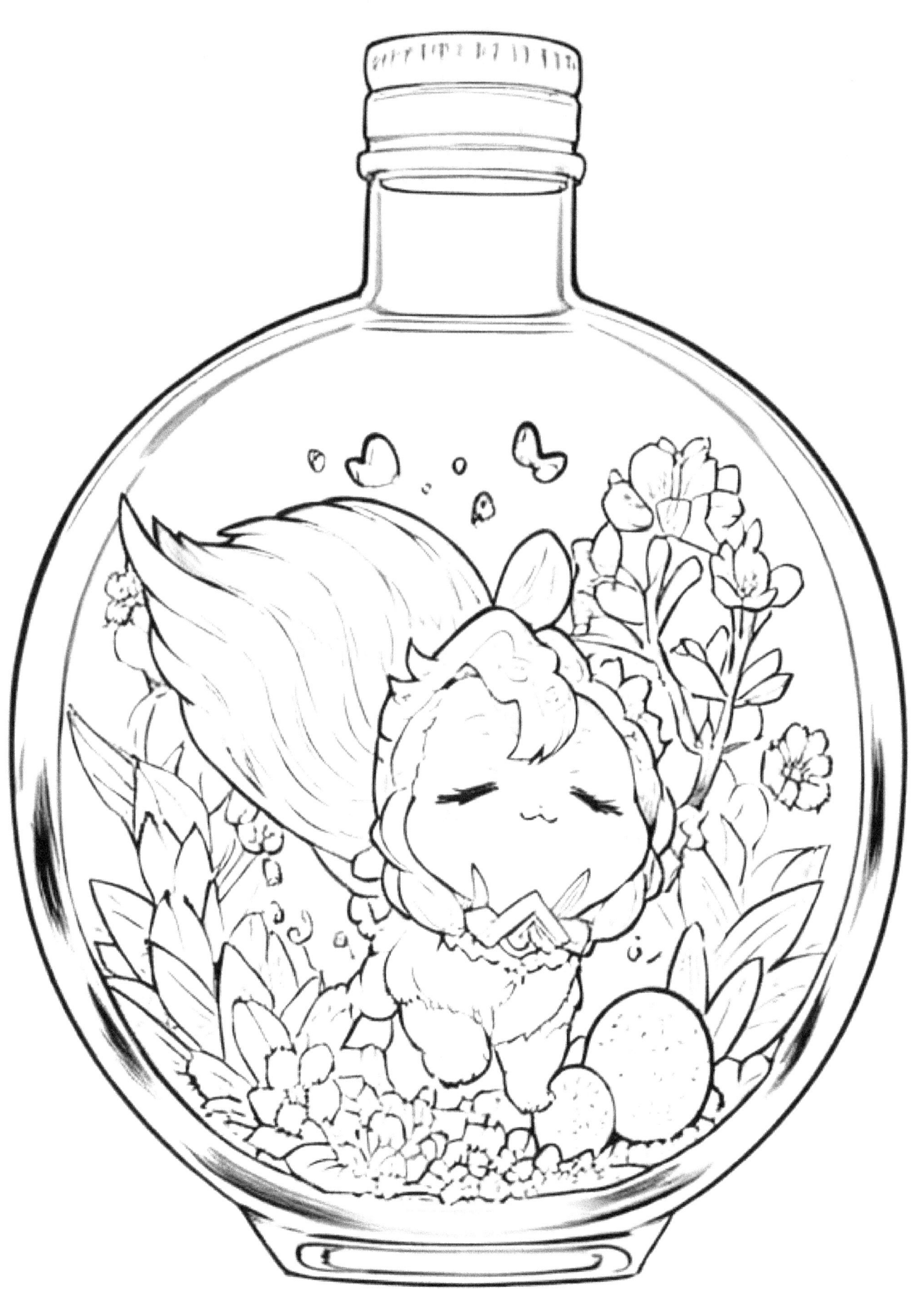

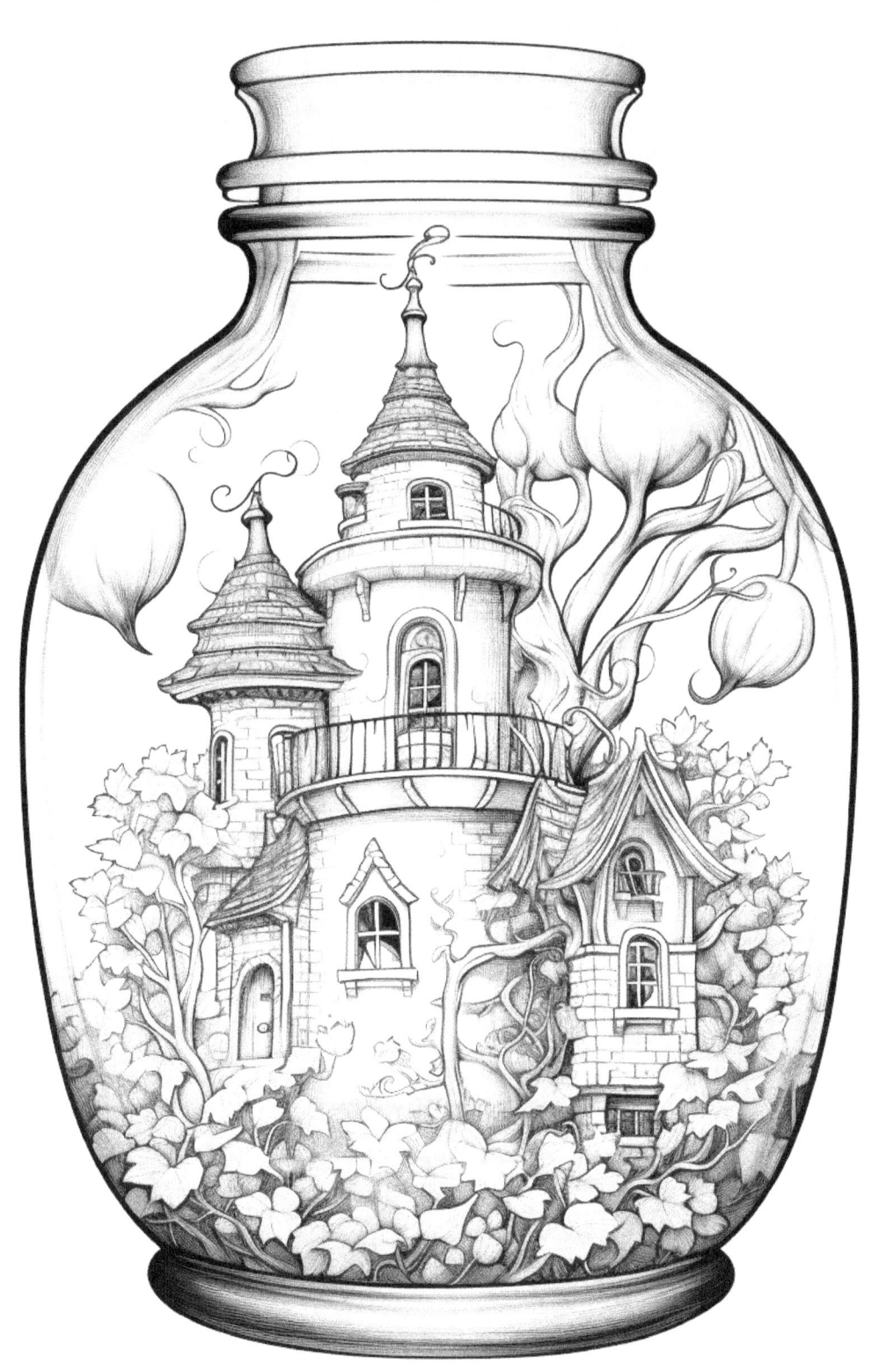

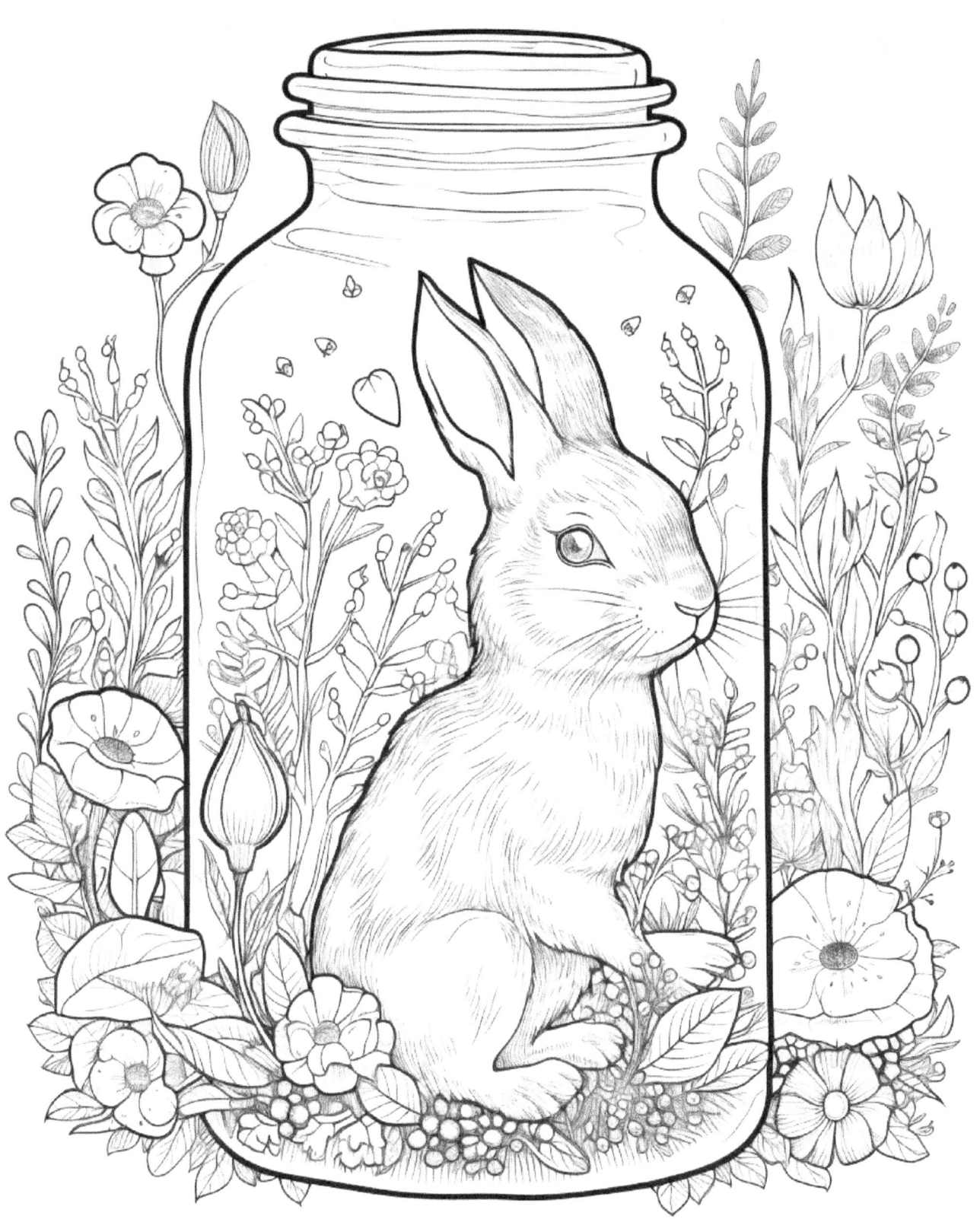

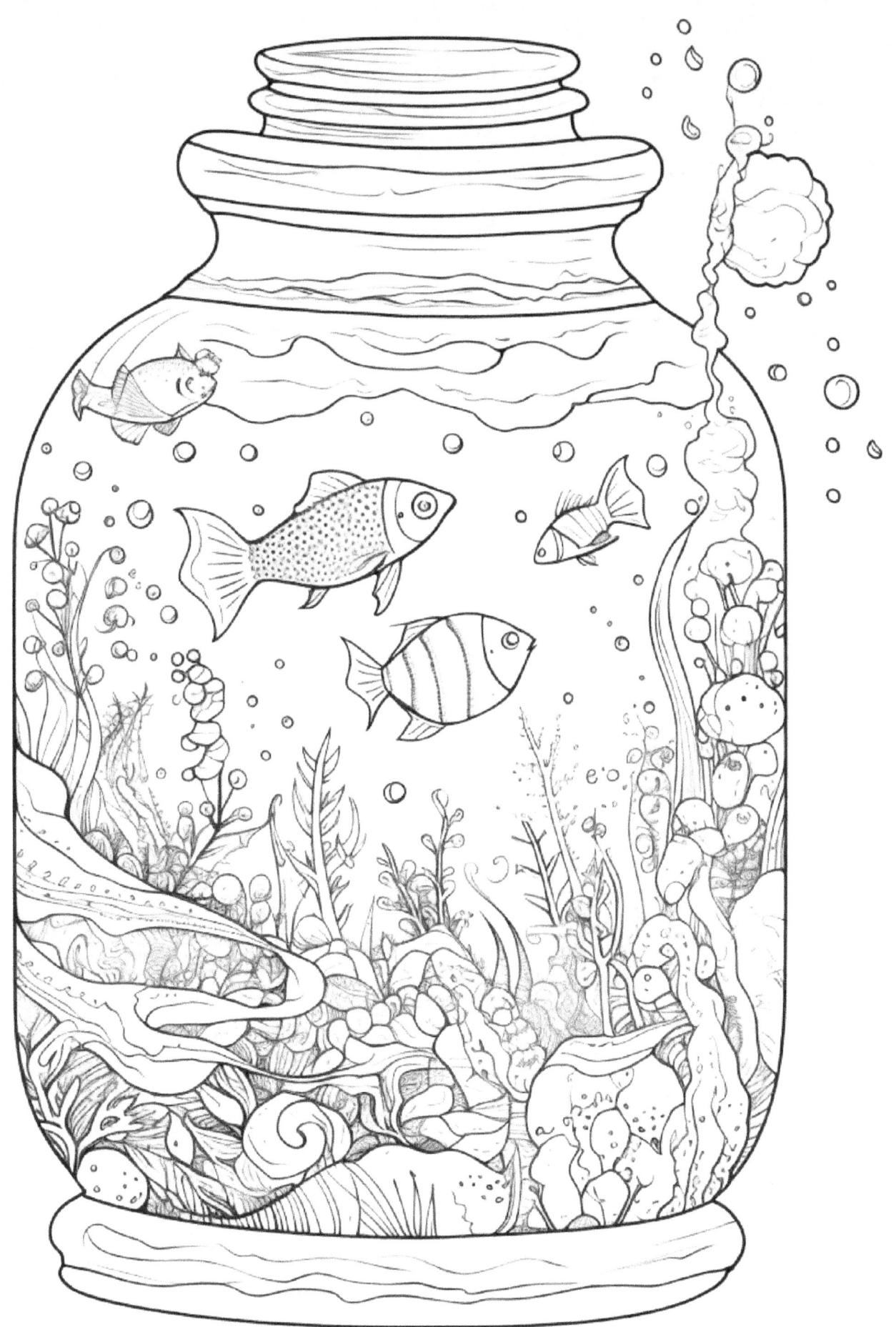

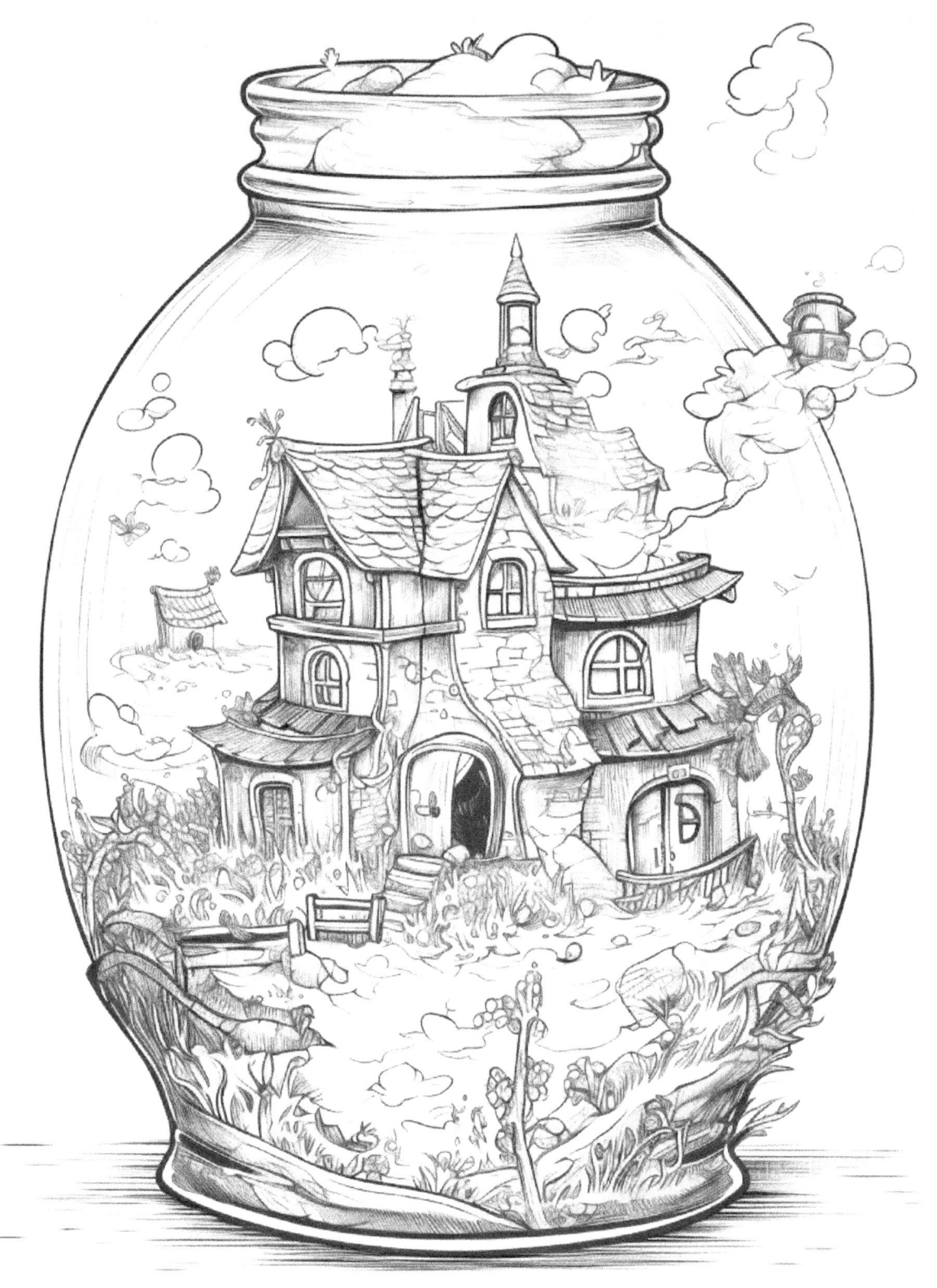

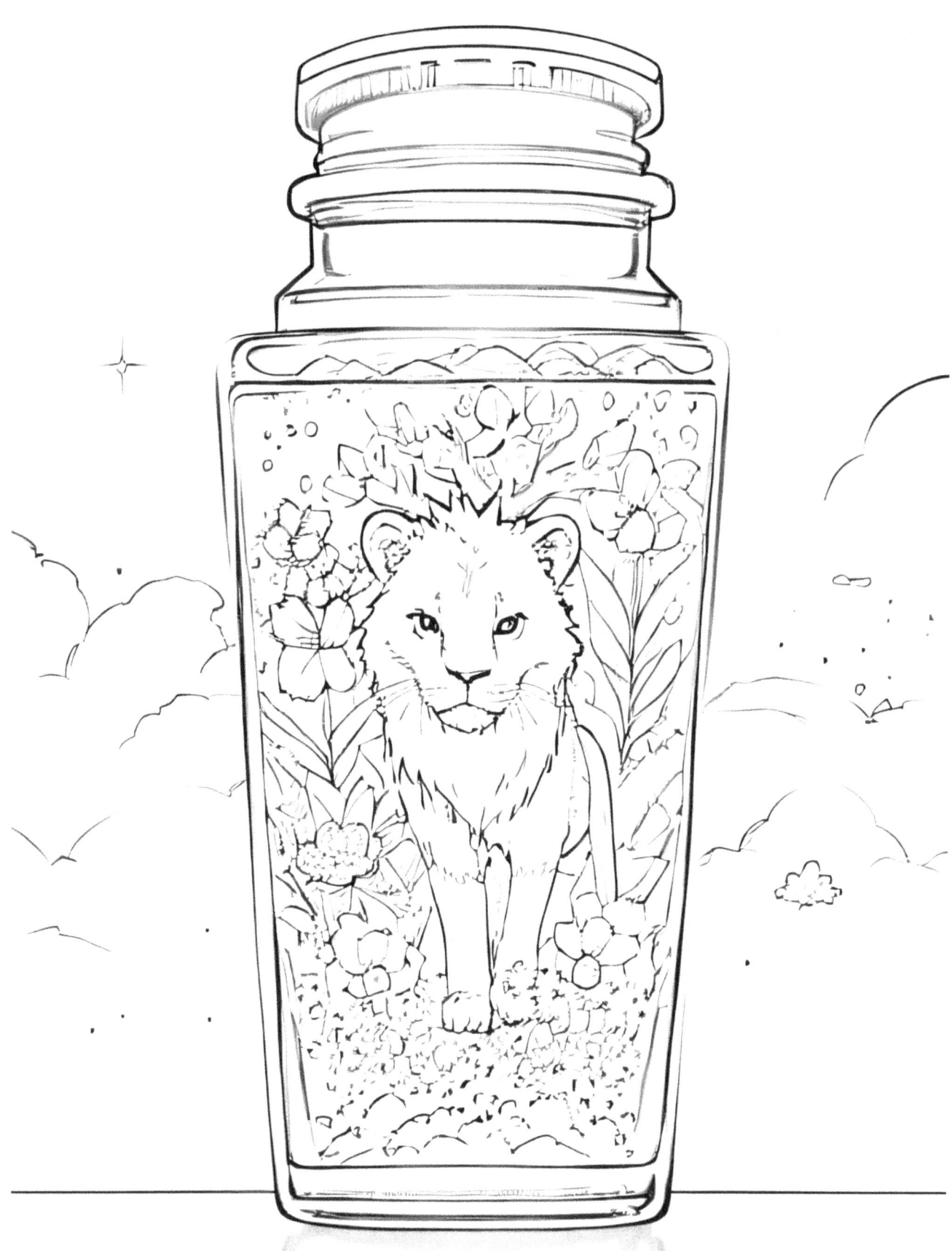

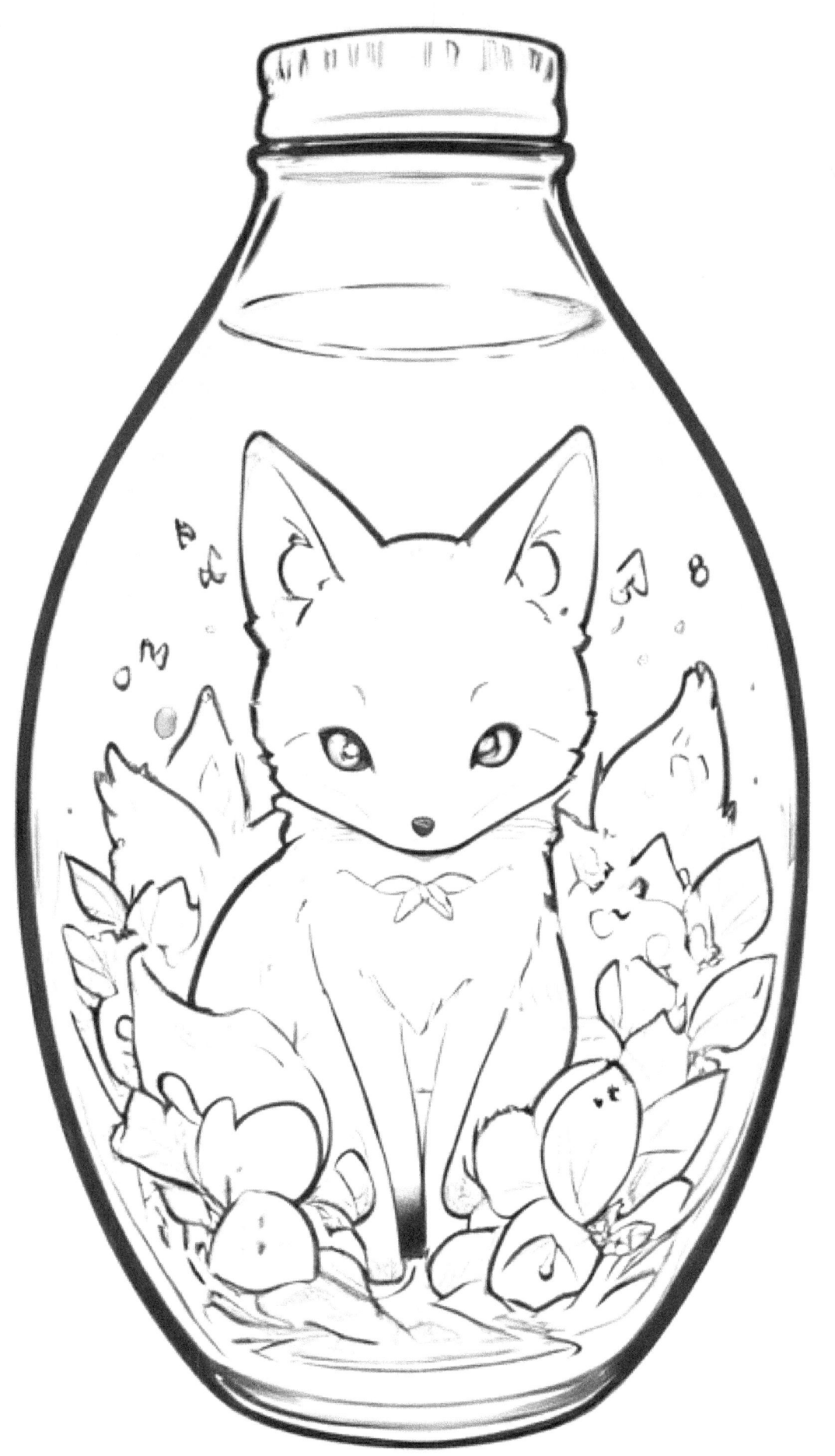

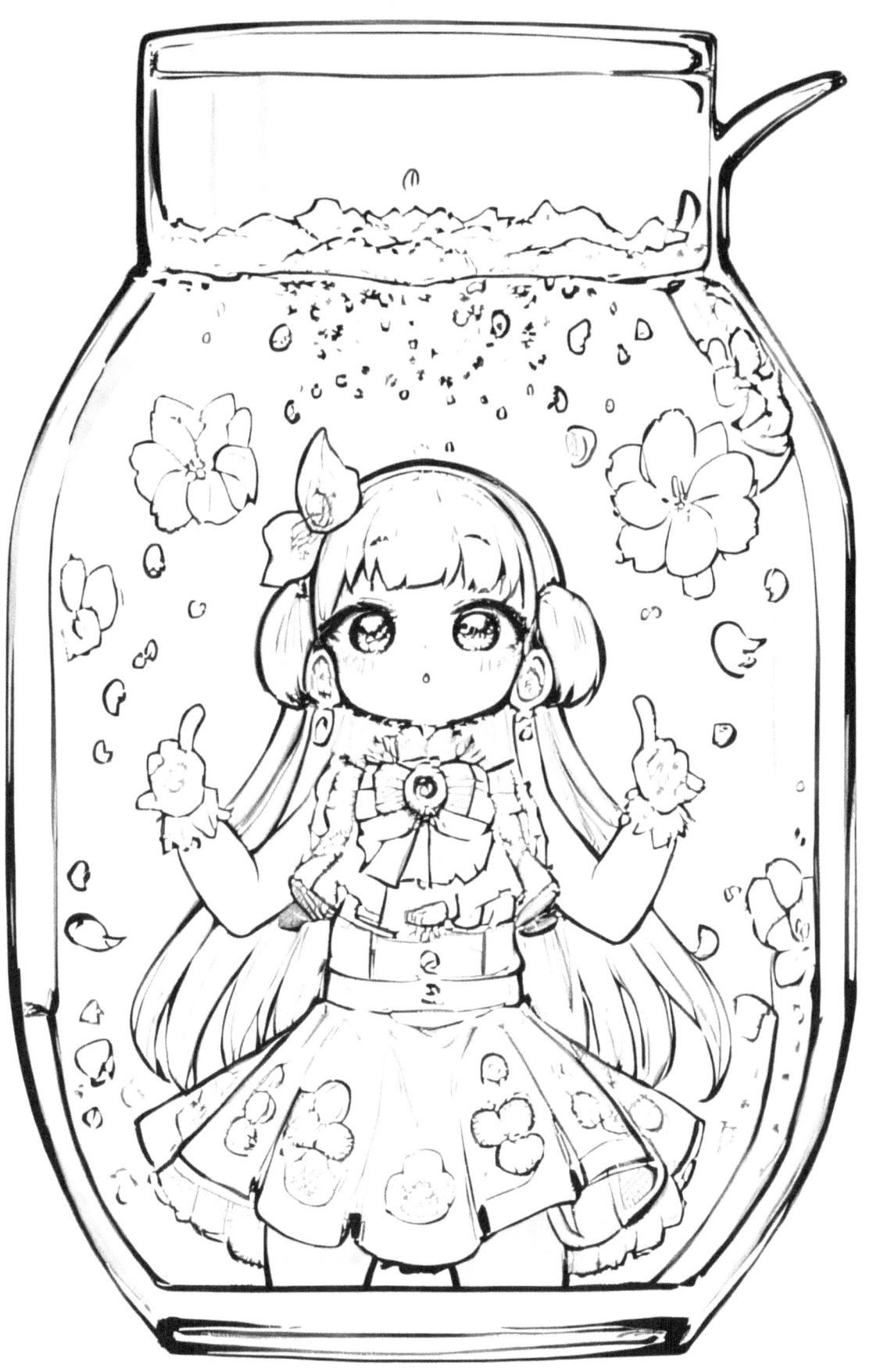

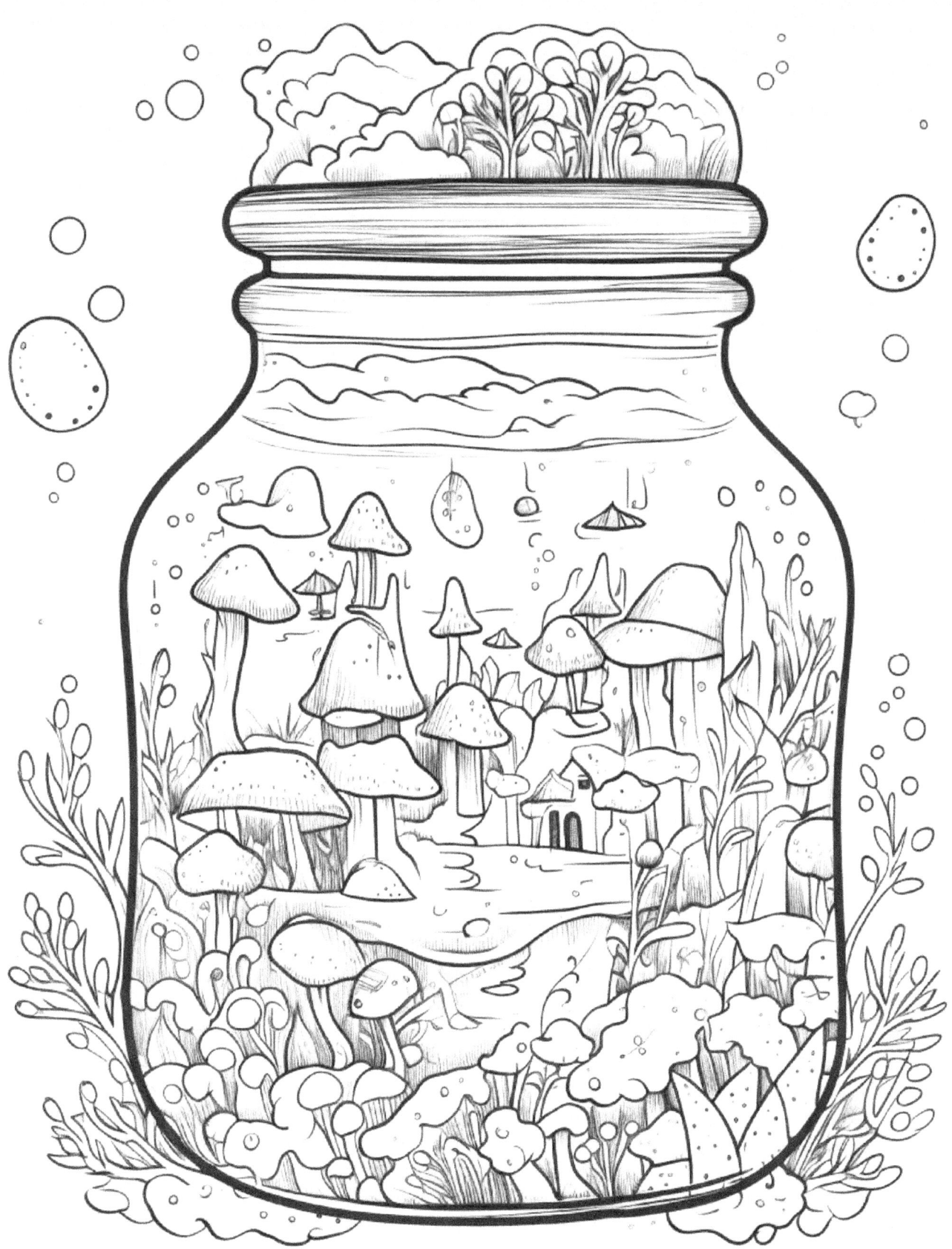

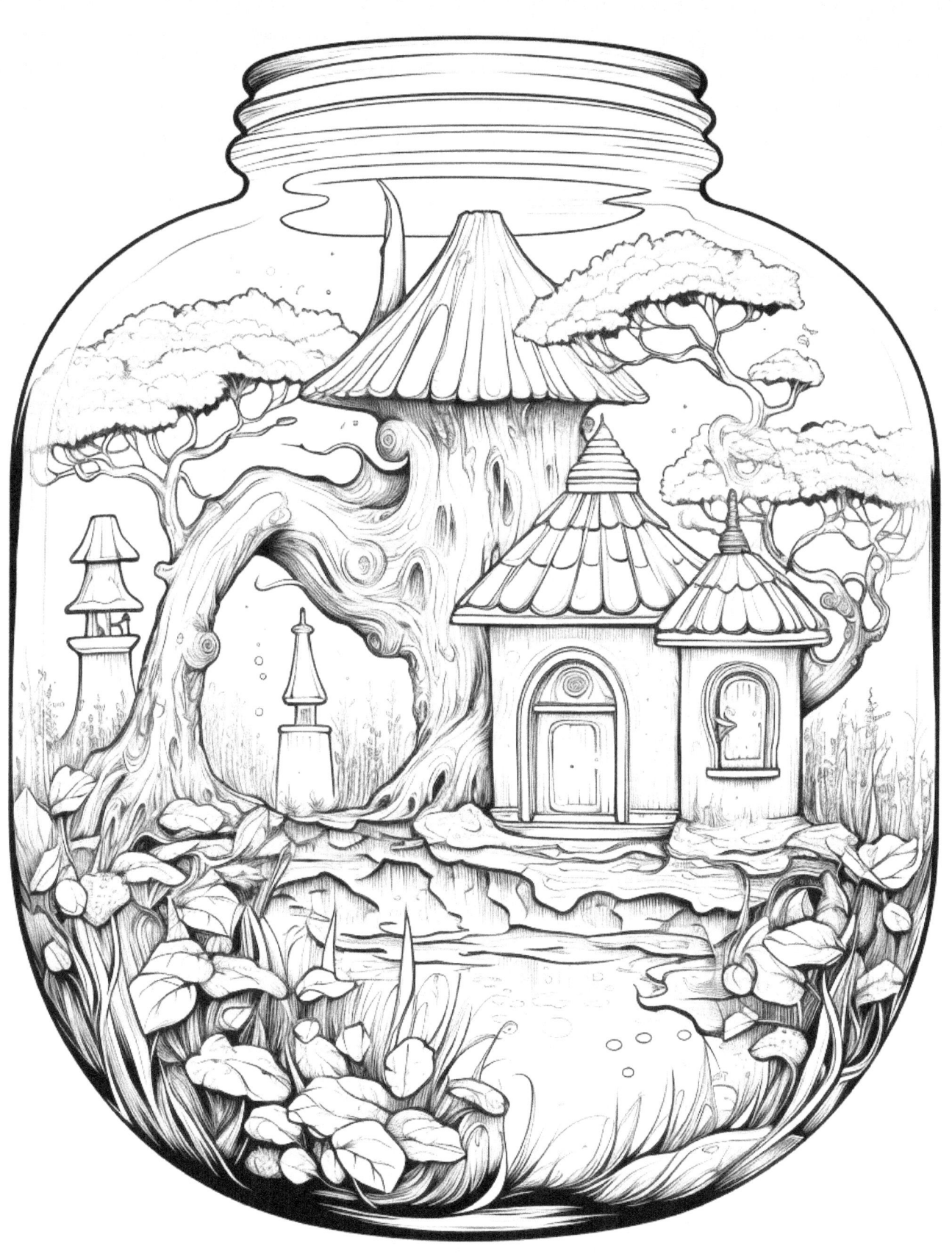

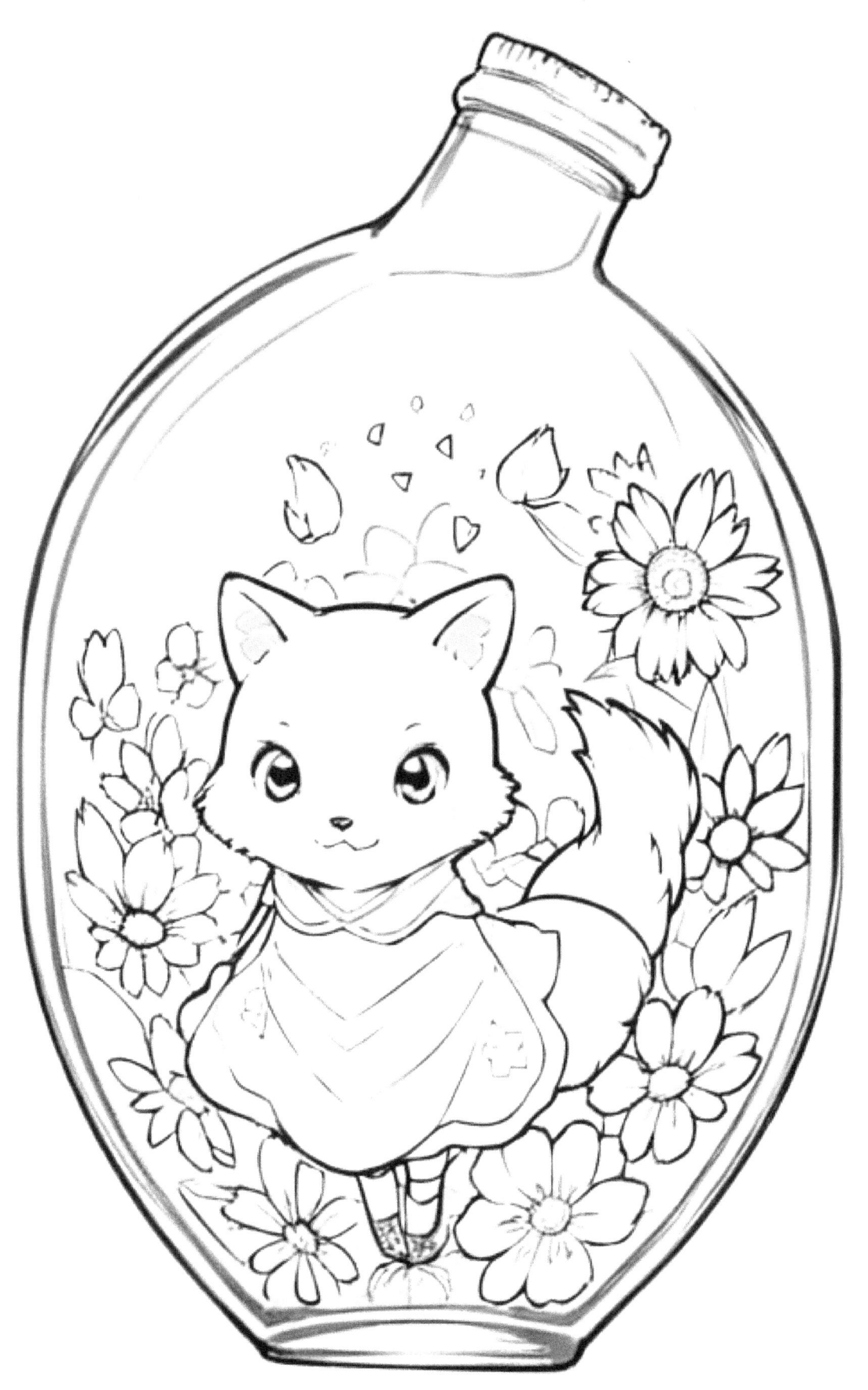

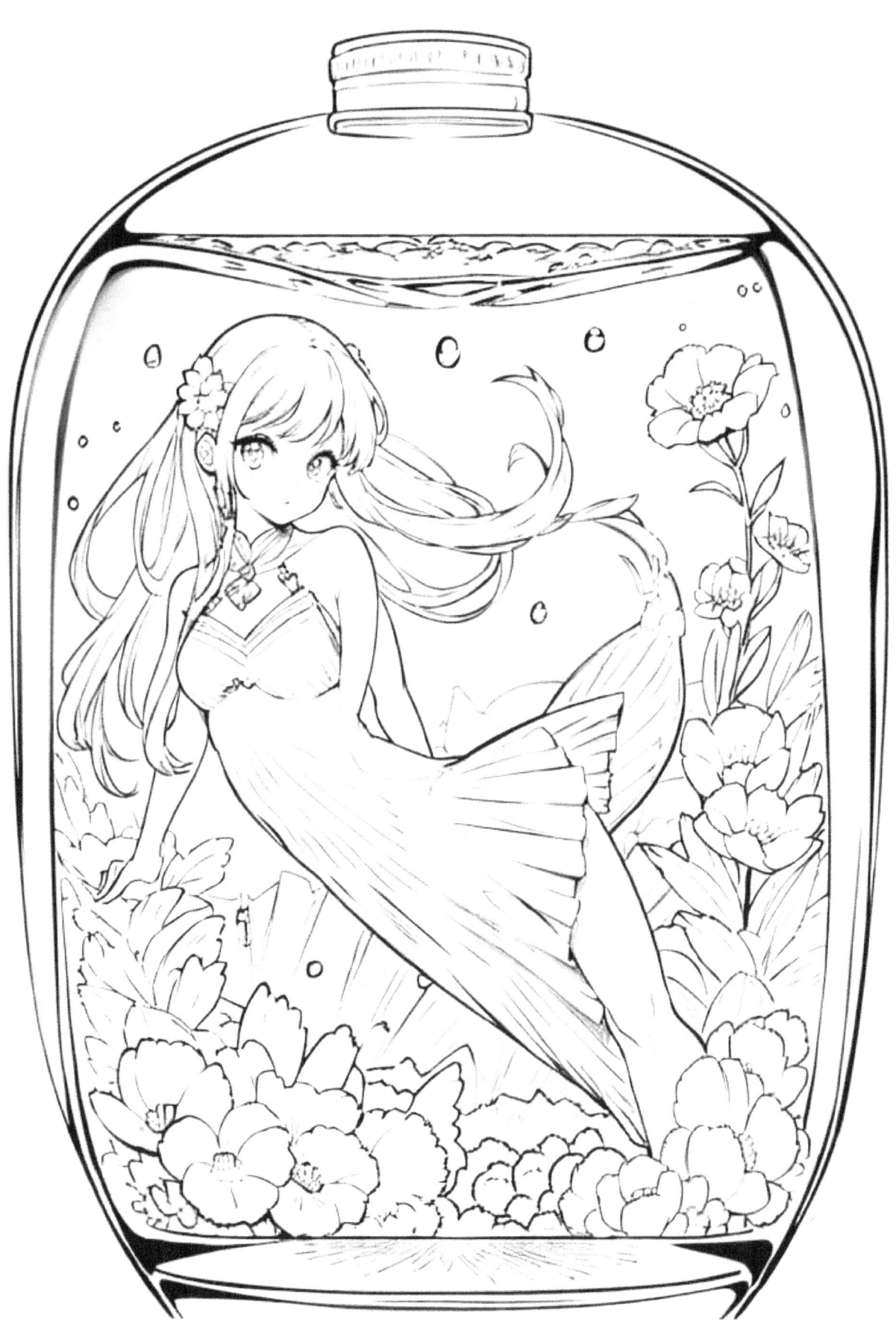

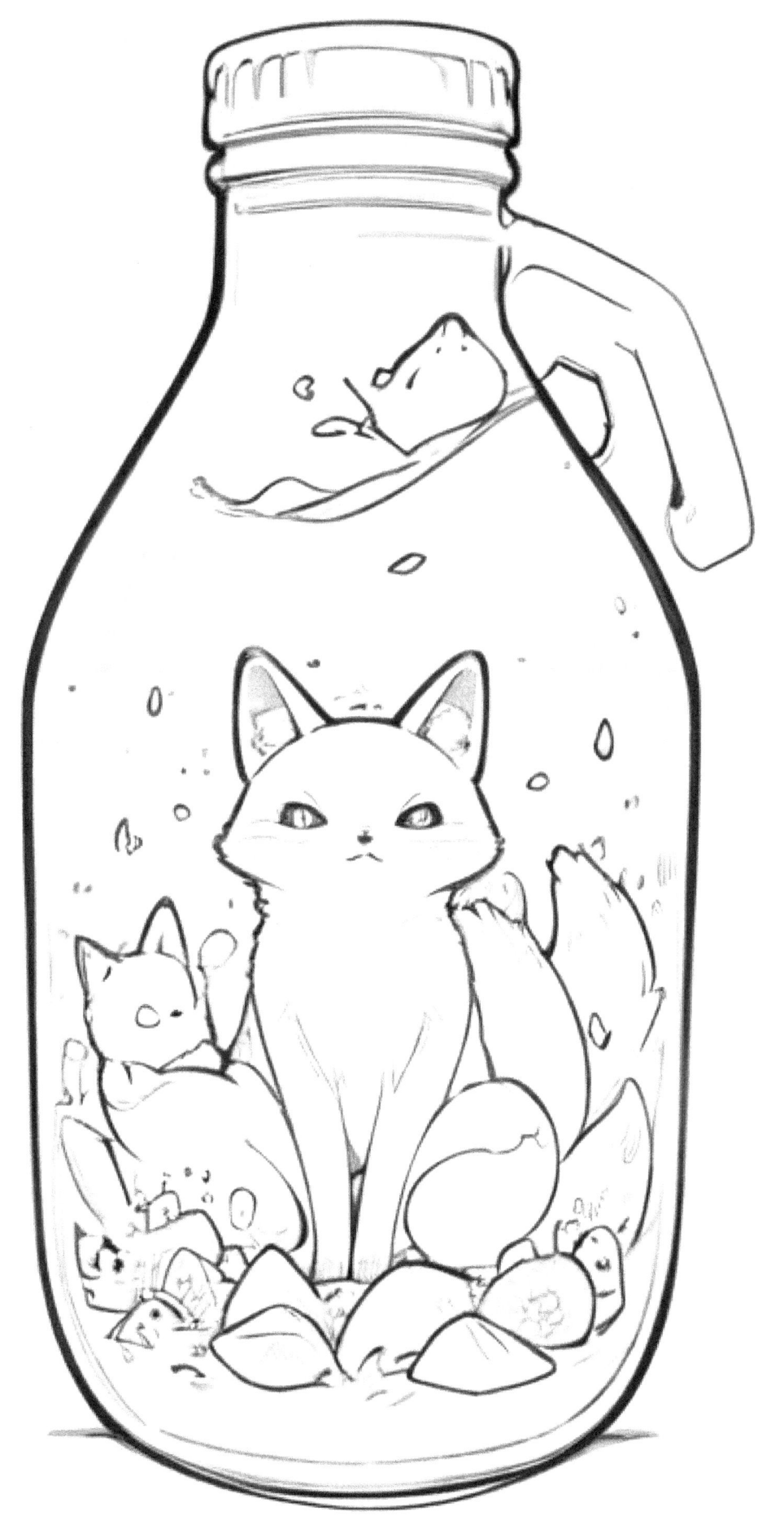

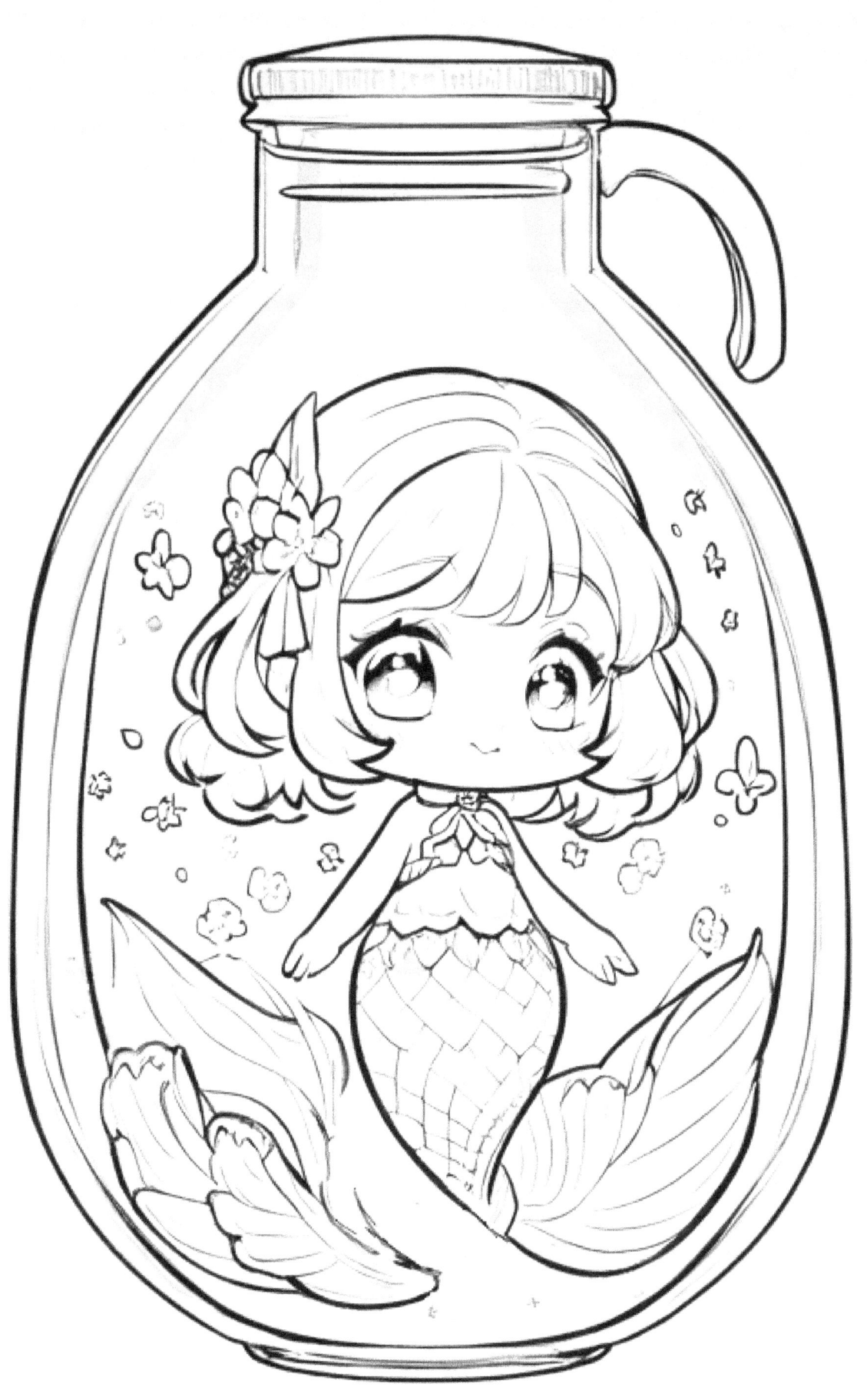

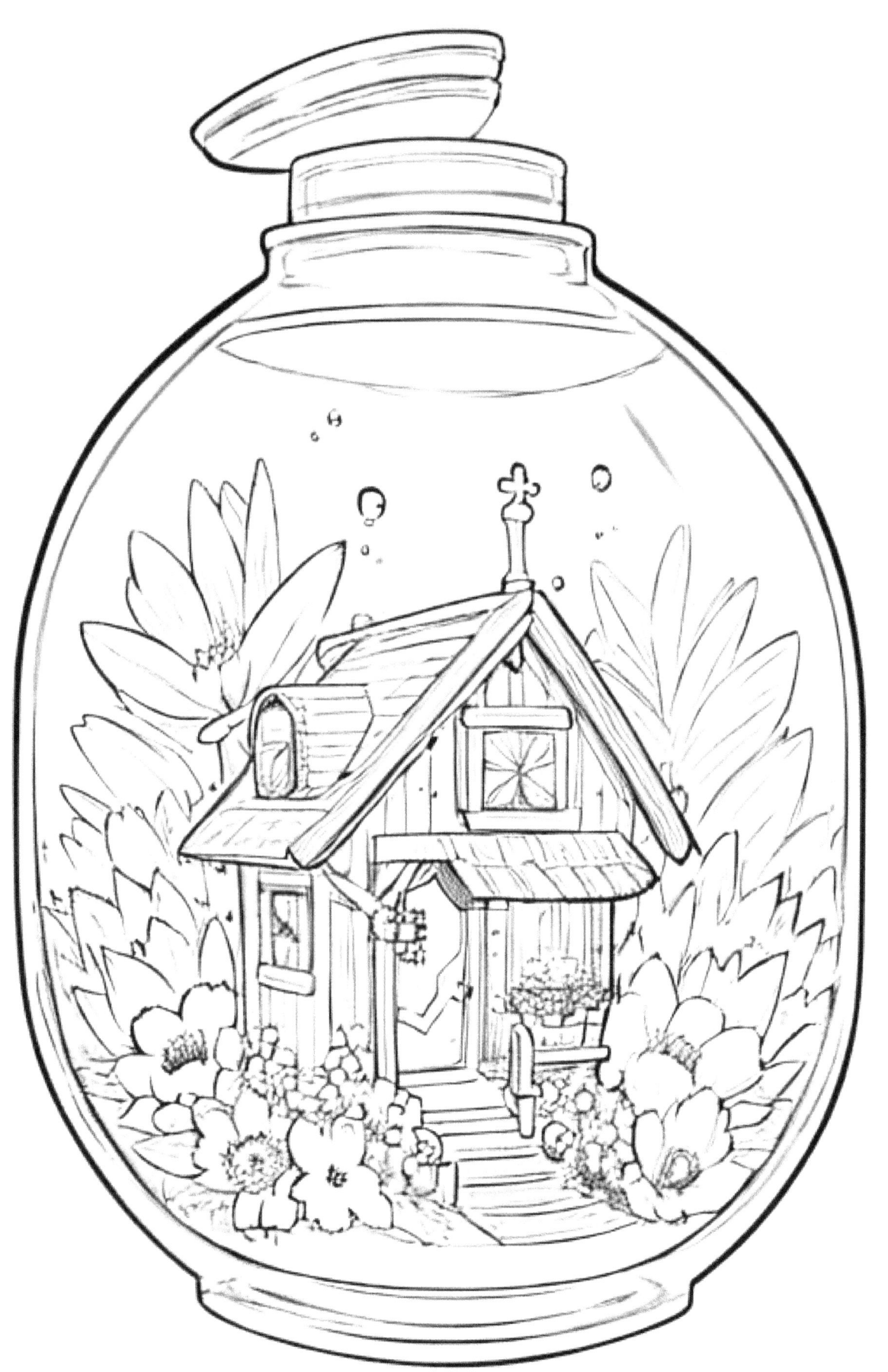

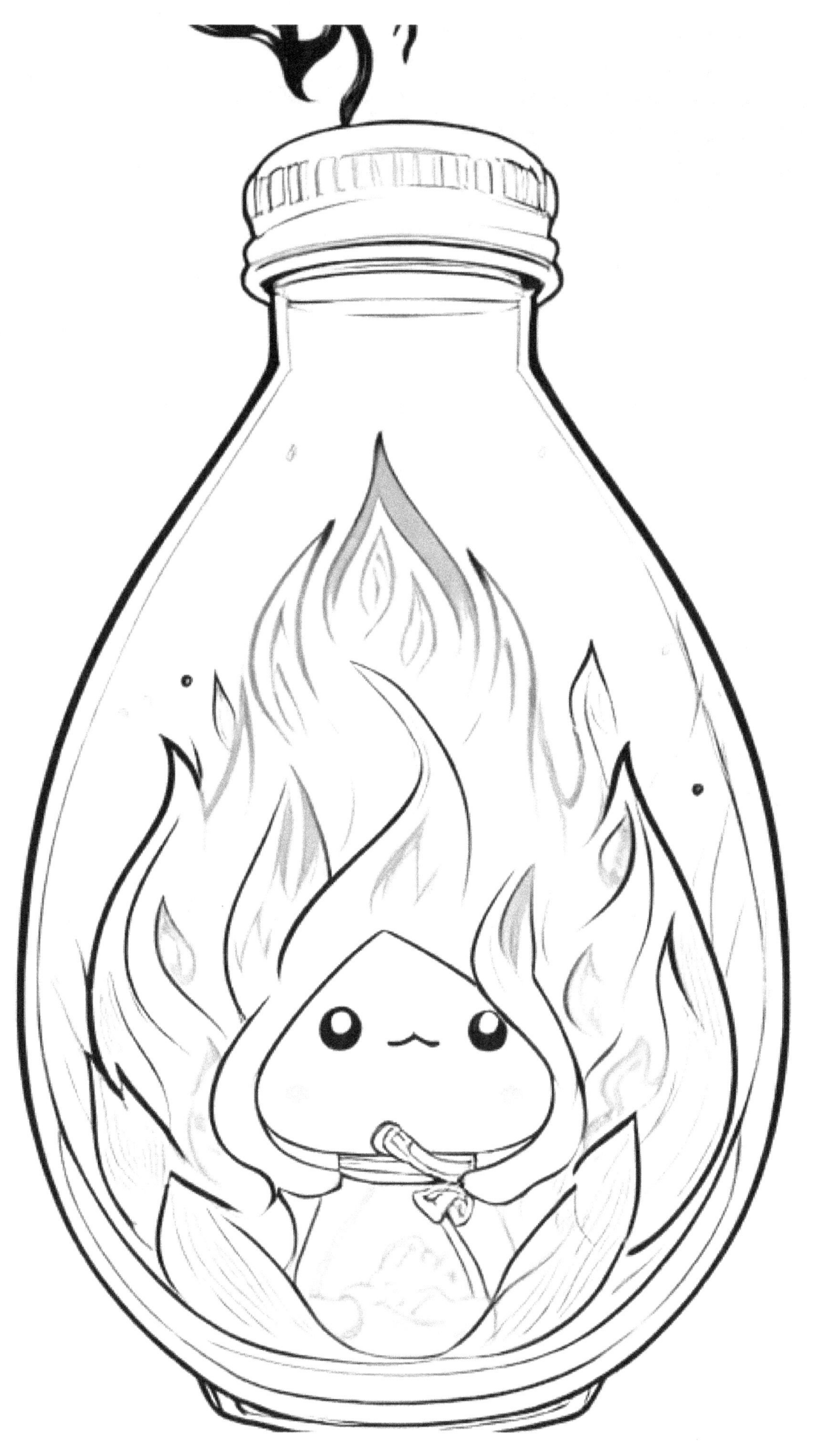

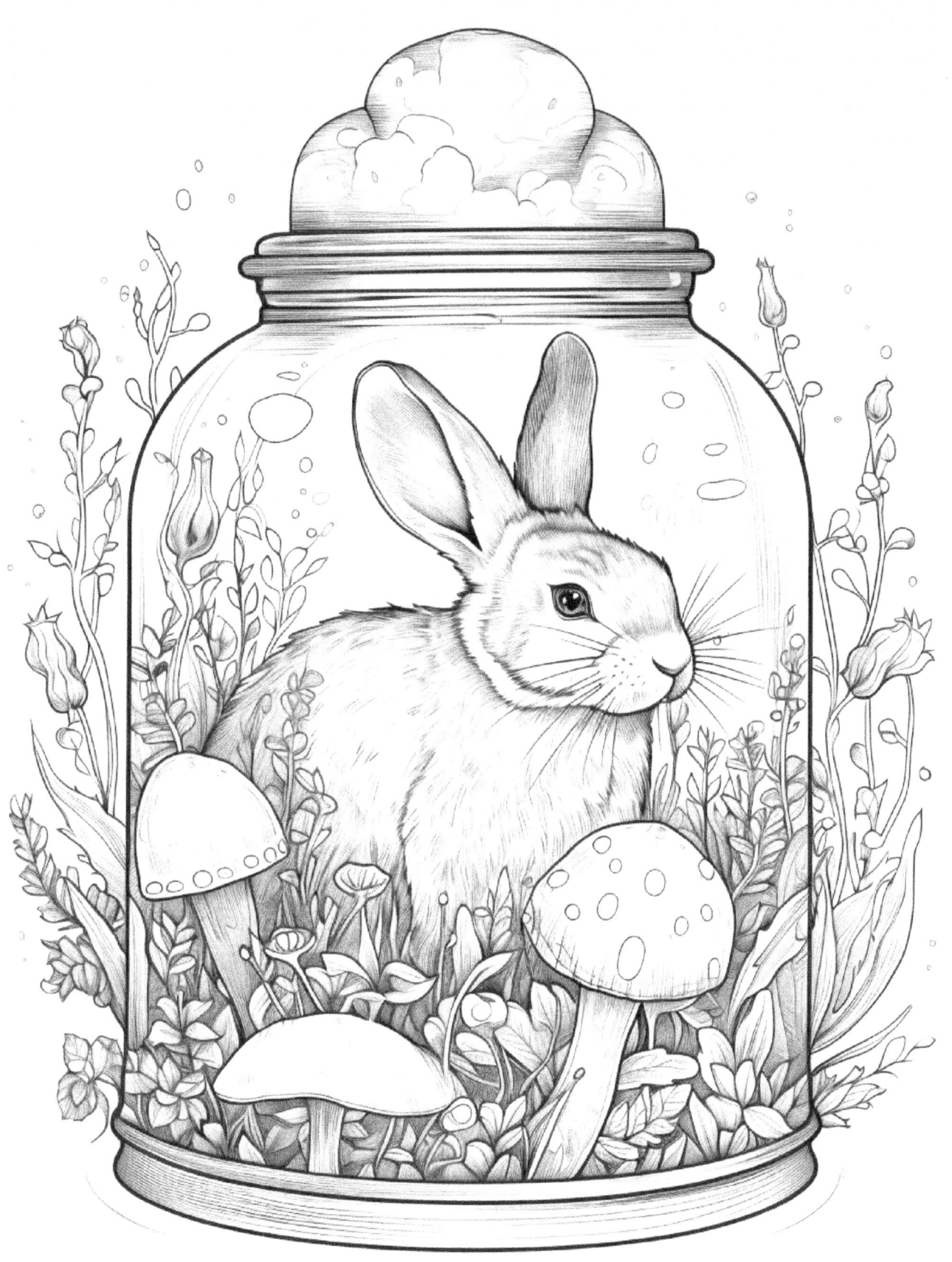

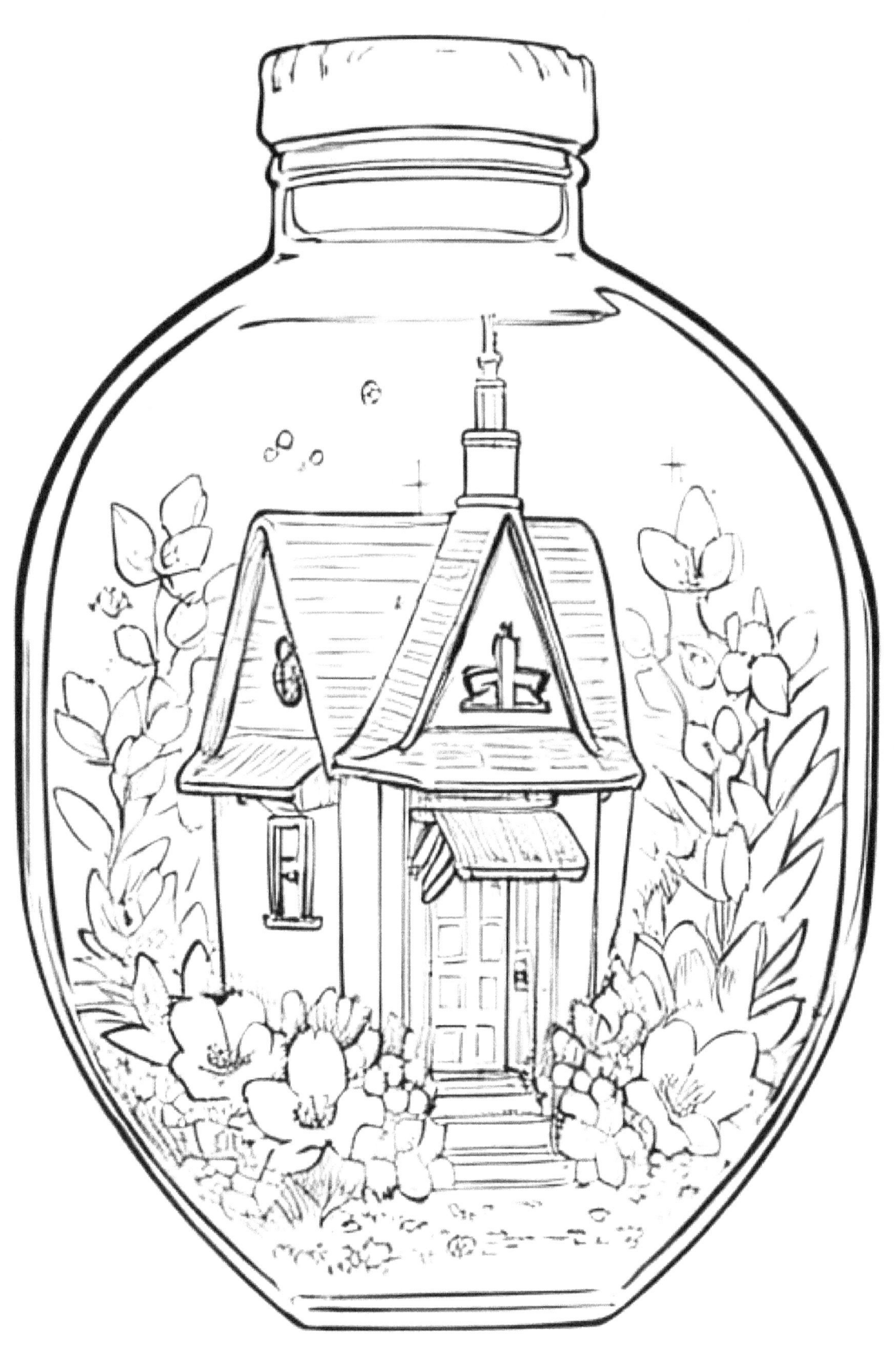

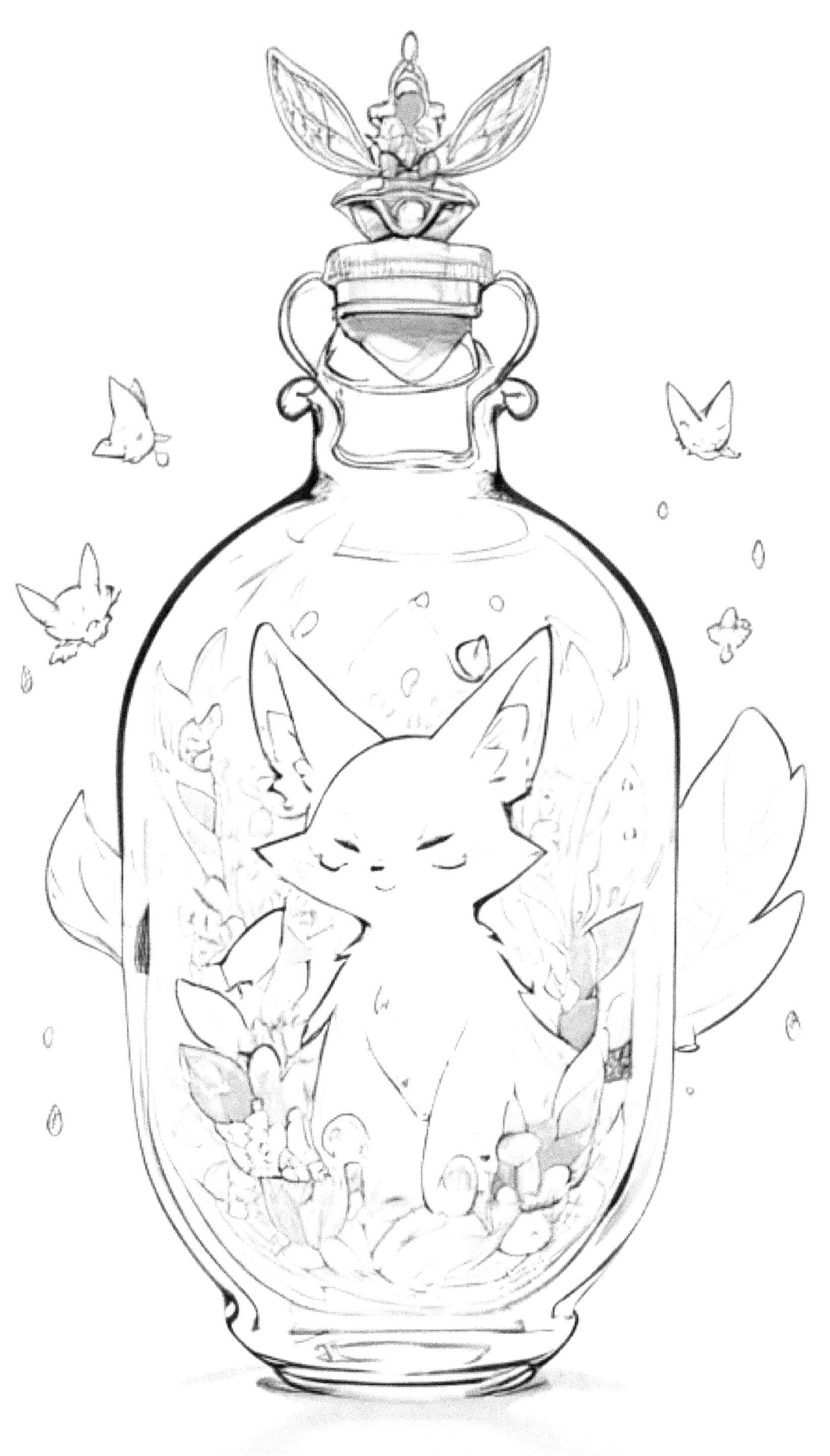

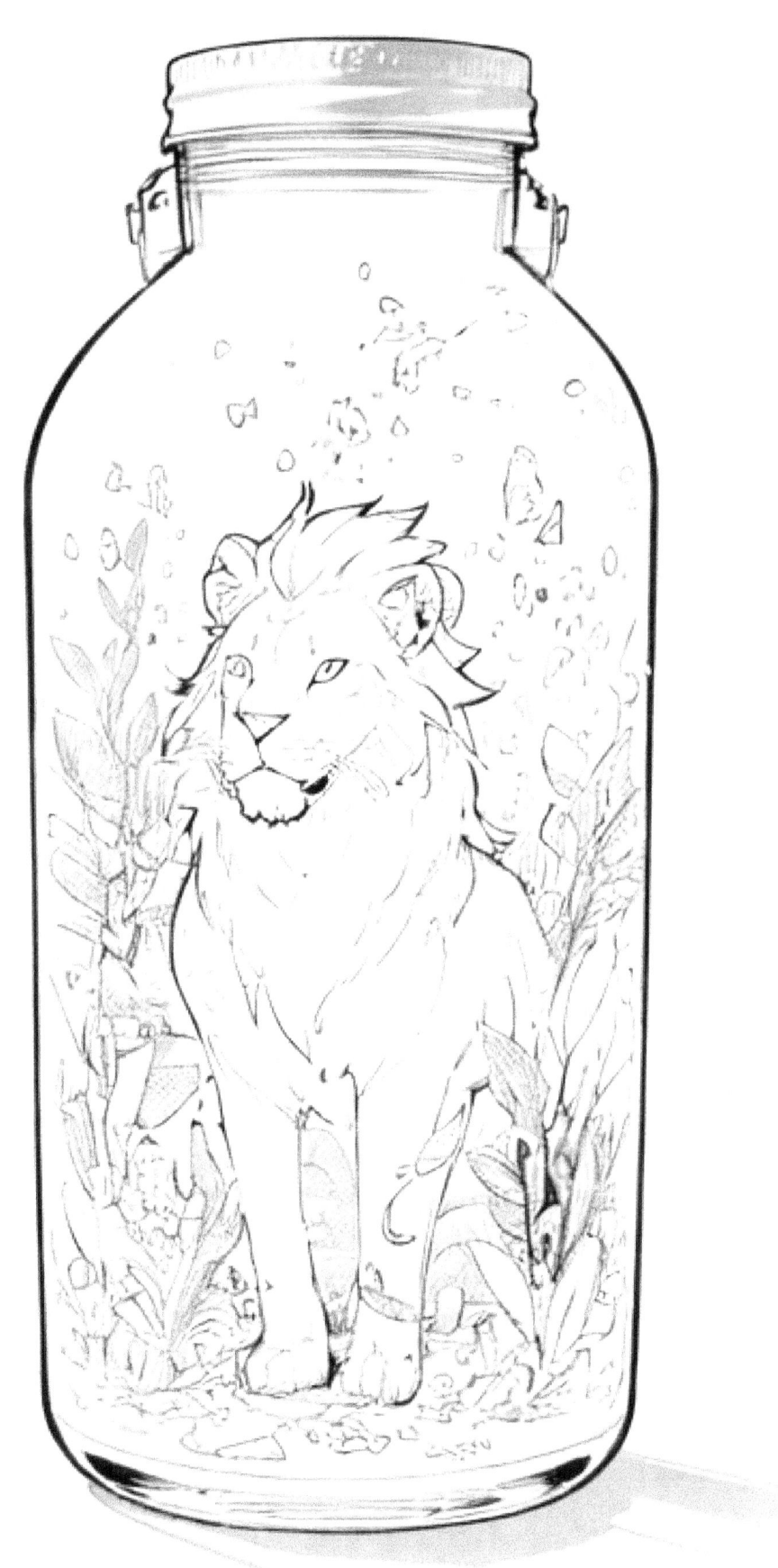

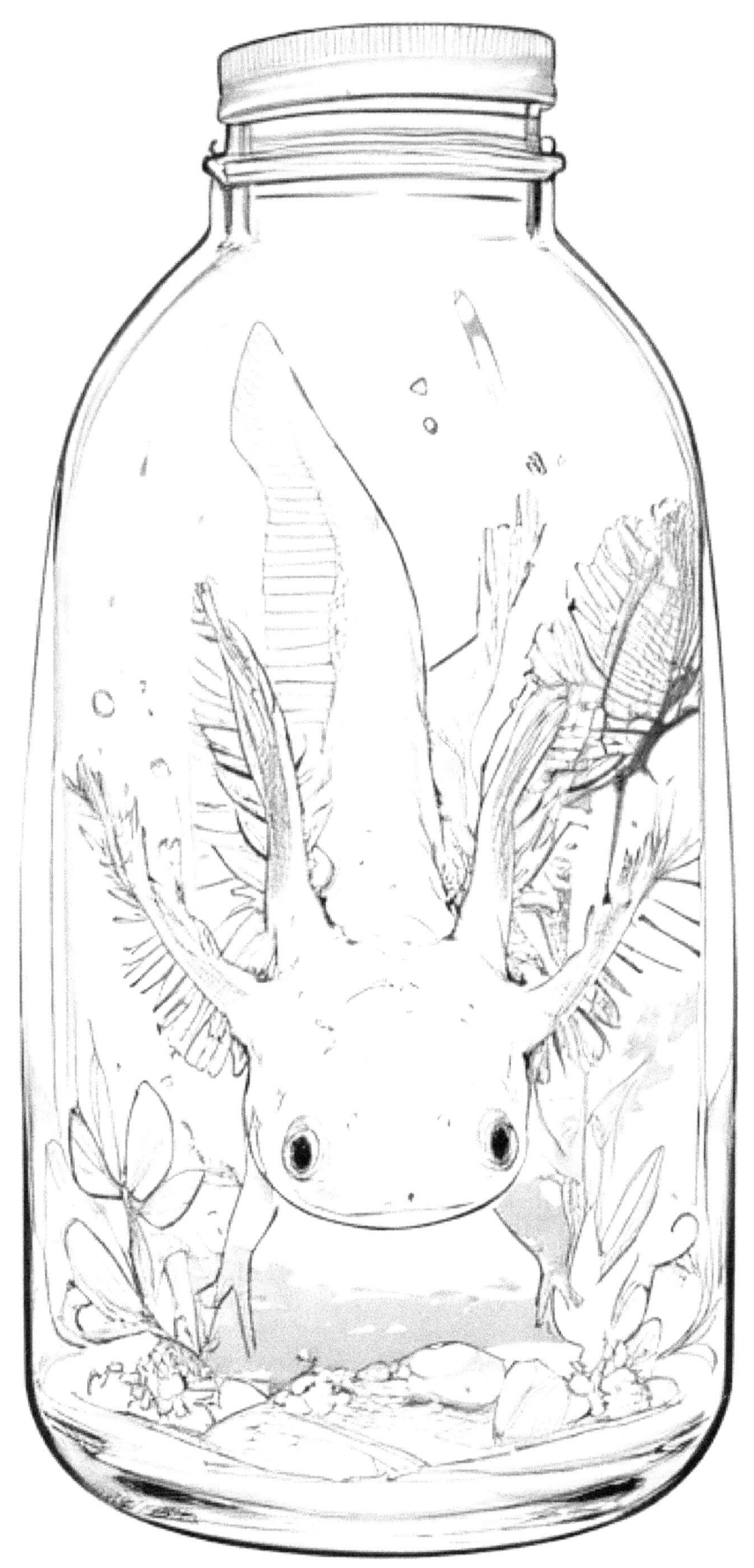

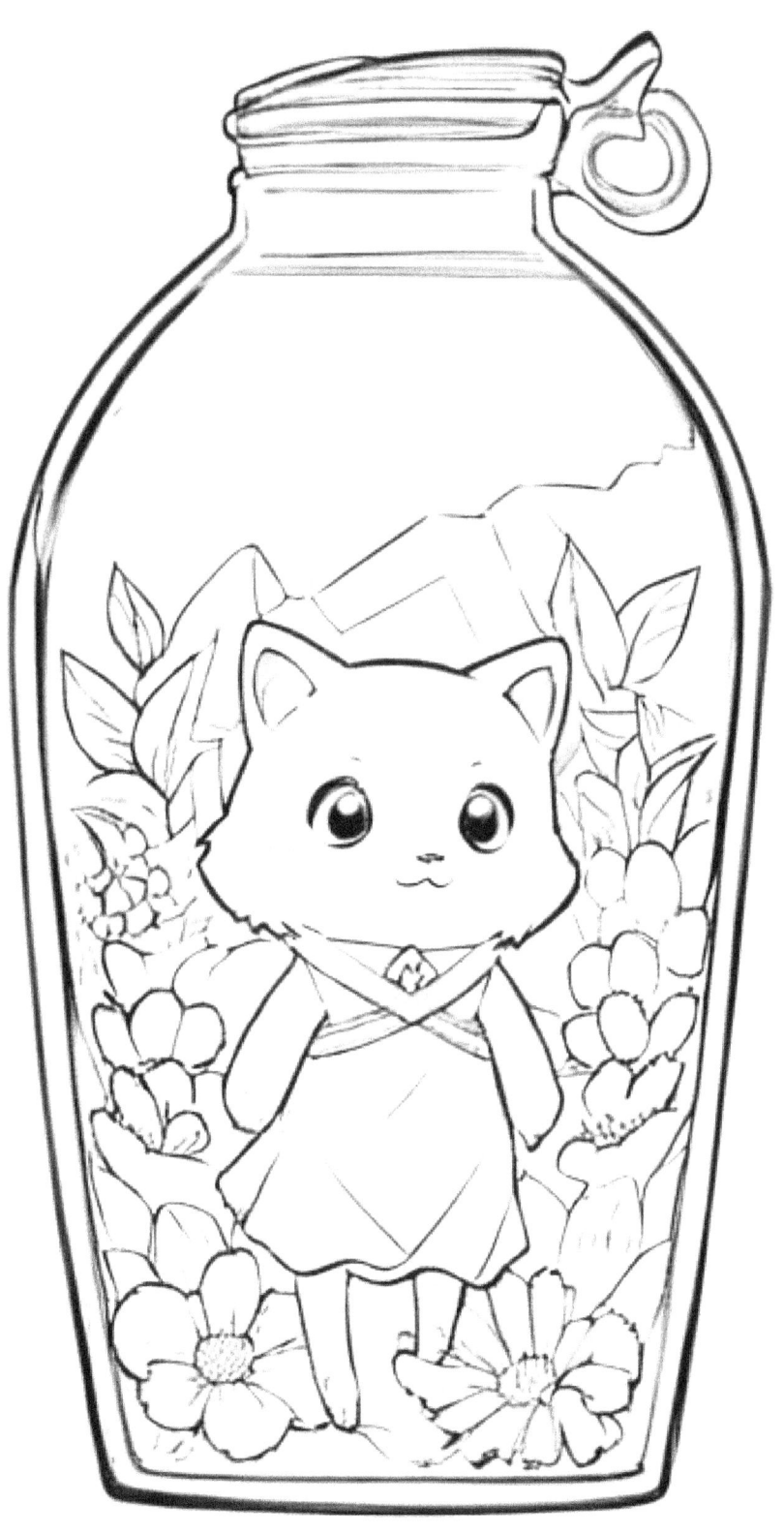

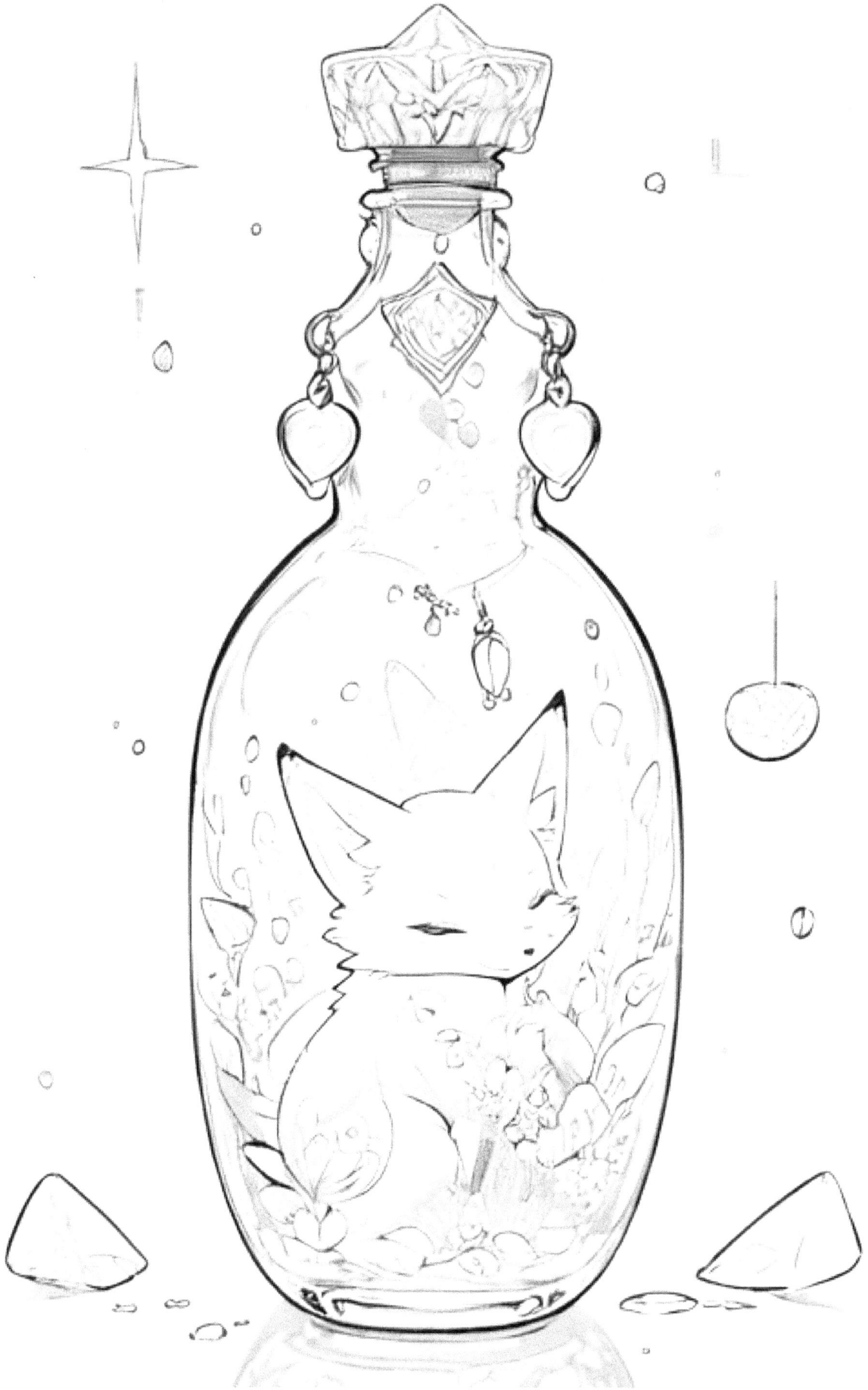

Thank You

Sankara Devi

www.ingramcontent.com/pod-product-compliance
Lightning Source LLC
Chambersburg PA
CBHW081134290526
45795CB00006B/2226